Broken, Changed and Rearranged

# What people are saying about Broken, Changed, and Rearranged

"*Broken, Changed, and Rearranged* takes readers on an empowering journey that shows people-pleasers: Your tendencies are not your destiny. This book is for every person who has suffered from the self-imposed shame of an imagined fatal mistake, who believes they aren't worthy unless others deem them so, and who craves the mental and emotional freedom of accepting their inherent value and expressing themselves authentically."

—**Maki Moussavi,** Executive Coach and
Author of *The High Achievers Guide*

"*Broken, Changed, and Rearranged* is an extremely relatable book that I found myself captivated by and saw myself in parts of her story. Through her prose, Liesl lets the reader know that they are not alone in their painful life experiences and provides such profound insights on beginning the healing process. Liesl makes it clear that we all have a story to tell and can always find the light at the end of every tunnel."

—**Ashley Taylor,** Entrepreneur, Coach, and
Founder of Gal with Anxiety Community

"This book is spot on! Liesl does an awesome job painting a picture to help you move forward from terror to freedom and take control of your life. This is not just a book, but a tool that really helps you to focus on what is the next right step for you to take to move forward when you're stuck in your difficult story. *Broken Changed, and Rearranged* is a powerful self-development guide to move you past your difficult story and start living again!"

—**Rynette Upson-Bush,** Speaker, Success Coach, Certified Educator, and Author of *Girl Get up and Move!*

LIESL HAYS

# Broken Changed & Rearranged

You Are Just One
Unbearable Truth Away from
the Next Person You Are Meant to Be

NEW YORK

LONDON • NASHVILLE • MELBOURNE • VANCOUVER

# Broken, Changed and Rearranged

You are Just One Unbearable Truth Away from the Next Person You are Meant to Be

Published in New York, New York, by Morgan James Publishing. Morgan James is a trademark of Morgan James, LLC. www.MorganJamesPublishing.com

**Morgan James BOGO™**

A **FREE** ebook edition is available for you or a friend with the purchase of this print book.

CLEARLY SIGN YOUR NAME ABOVE

**Instructions to claim your free ebook edition:**
1. Visit MorganJamesBOGO.com
2. Sign your name CLEARLY in the space above
3. Complete the form and submit a photo of this entire page
4. You or your friend can download the ebook to your preferred device

ISBN 9781631955624 paperback
ISBN 9781631955631 ebook
Library of Congress Control Number: 2021934468

**Cover & Interior Design by:**
Christopher Kirk
www.GFSstudio.com

**Morgan James PUBLISHING Builds** with... **Habitat for Humanity® Peninsula and Greater Williamsburg**

Morgan James is a proud partner of Habitat for Humanity Peninsula and Greater Williamsburg. Partners in building since 2006.

Get involved today! Visit
MorganJamesPublishing.com/giving-back

*Daddy, thank you for encouraging*
*this dream inside me since I was a little girl.*
*Harlen, this is our book.*
*Thank you for co-creating it with me. I love you.*
*Mady, Ethan, Mom, and Marta,*
*for loving me through each evolution.*

# Table of Contents

Acknowledgments . . . . . . . . . . . . . . . . . . . . . . . . . . . . xi
Preface . . . . . . . . . . . . . . . . . . . . . . . . . . . . . . . . . . . xiii
The Beginning . . . . . . . . . . . . . . . . . . . . . . . . . . . . . . xiv

**Part I: Broken** . . . . . . . . . . . . . . . . . . . . . . . . . . . . . .1
I used to Rule the World . . . . . . . . . . . . . . . . . . . . . . . .3
Crisis . . . . . . . . . . . . . . . . . . . . . . . . . . . . . . . . . . . . . .15
The Historic Browning . . . . . . . . . . . . . . . . . . . . . . . . .31
Own Your story . . . . . . . . . . . . . . . . . . . . . . . . . . . . . .47
Pain . . . . . . . . . . . . . . . . . . . . . . . . . . . . . . . . . . . . . . .59
Crisis-Proof Friendships . . . . . . . . . . . . . . . . . . . . . . . .73
Real . . . . . . . . . . . . . . . . . . . . . . . . . . . . . . . . . . . . . . .85

**Part II: Changed** . . . . . . . . . . . . . . . . . . . . . . . . . . . .95
What Got You Here, Won't Get You There . . . . . . . . . . .97
Discounts . . . . . . . . . . . . . . . . . . . . . . . . . . . . . . . . . .115
Toxic Truths . . . . . . . . . . . . . . . . . . . . . . . . . . . . . . .131
Unimportant Voices . . . . . . . . . . . . . . . . . . . . . . . . . .147

**Part III: Rearranged** . . . . . . . . . . . . . . . . . . . . . . . .163
Funeral Goals . . . . . . . . . . . . . . . . . . . . . . . . . . . . . .165
Trampoline Freedom . . . . . . . . . . . . . . . . . . . . . . . . .177

Let's Write Our Stories Together . . . . . . . . . . . . . . . . .185
About the Author . . . . . . . . . . . . . . . . . . . . . . . . . . . .187

# Acknowledgments

*H*arlen, for supporting me in sharing our story out loud so others can heal and for loving me back first.

Mady and Chinny, for showing me what it means to love someone even when others think they are "ugly".

Ethan, for always knowing exactly what to say encouraging me to move forward.

Daddy, for always saying "Liesy, I've always said you need to write a book one day. You are an incredible writer."

Mom, for always correcting my spelling, grammar, and general punctuation. Look at us now.

Marta, for keeping my secret for so long as I processed through my healing. We are opposites in the best way.

Eugene, you were my bestest dog friend. Your sudden death reminded me that our time on this earth can be cut short inspiring me to finish this book.

Lily, my beloved goldendoodle, thank you for always giving me sloppy kisses at all the right moments.

Bear, for reminding me that I could love another dog again. You are the best parts of all the dogs I have ever loved.

Pawpaw, for living a life that beautifully encapsulates all my funeral goals.

Uncle T, for writing a eulogy that inspired our whole family. Thank you for letting me use it.

Trisha, for editing each word with me. This book was a true partnership.

Maki, for being a divine truth-teller. Thank you for loving me enough to always tell me the truth. You are my dearest friend.

Jodi, you are a stunning friend. Thank you for loving me when most people walked out. Your passion for love and healing inspires me.

Melissa W., for always being willing to roll up your sleeves and co-create with me. I'm so fortunate to call you a friend.

Nick, for always being willing to ask the hard questions and dig in deep. You're one of my favorite humans.

Melissa O, for working through my story with me and helping me heal. The moment we met, I knew our lives would be forever connected.

Julie and Mike, for always making me feel important.

True North, my divine and wise inner voice, thank you for reminding me never to abandon myself. You are my truest guide and mentor. I love you more than you know.

# Preface

This wasn't the book I was supposed to write. I never planned on telling this story out loud. It was to remain hidden and never spoken of again. It was my narrative to control, and I wanted to keep it safe. The mere thought of sharing the worst thing about myself with the world made me want to vomit.

I had everything planned out perfectly. I was going to write a leadership book that focused on the behaviors people needed to possess when approaching change. It was going to propel my Human Resources consulting business to the next level. I conducted interviews with several influential leaders, asking them to codify their approach to change. I started a deep qualitative analysis that occupied hours of my life. My book was scientific, unemotional and uninspiring. I was 20,000-plus words deep into my manuscript, but when I read it out loud, I was unmoved. After all I had invested in it, I expected to feel something. Despite my lack of emotion, I was intent on moving forward. I remember saying, "Perhaps, I'll write a book I'm passionate about next time."

The universe had different plans for my life.

Every time I focused on the leadership manuscript, the topic of the current book you are holding began to surface. I fought with myself for months about sharing this story out loud. The book I wanted to write for my ego and the one I was supposed to write were battling for attention. I fought with my deep inner voice for months.

After a full-day writing session that went nowhere, I sat on my porch and cried. I placed my hands up into the air and yelled out loud, "What do you want from me? To tell the worst thing about myself out loud? Why do you want that from me?"

I was an inconsolable mess who desperately wanted to escape sharing the most embarrassing story of my life.

As I ugly cried on my deck, my deep inner voice whispered, "Healing."

After that day, the decision to give life to this book became a reality. It was not easy, and I would be lying if I told you I enjoyed the entire process. There were places I had to revisit that I never wanted to go back to.

Beloved, we all have stories we keep locked away. Some of these stories are meant to help set others free. Here I am. All of me. Sharing one of the hardest parts of my journey with you out loud because I believe it will set both of us free.

Are you ready? I'm still not sure I am.

However, I believe we can do difficult things together.

Let's do a difficult thing together.

Okay, I'm ready now.

## The Beginning

The day after I quit my corporate job at one of the largest global healthcare IT companies in the world, I was standing in my shower thinking it was an accomplishment that I had even managed to get out of bed that day. Marinating in my own misery was threatening to become an all-day state of being.

As the hot shower water hit my head that morning, I felt two emotions: freedom mixed with complete and absolute terror stemming from the belief my entire life was destroyed. I had spent the past ten years of my life laser-focused on crushing every neatly predefined ambition society had placed on me. I was married to a man who adored me by the time I was twenty-four, had two babies by the time I was twenty-seven, and attained a career for which anyone would be envious.

Each time I achieved one of these goals, I ravenously hungered for more because I never felt full. I had made the dangerous assumption that I only needed to achieve the next admirable milestone to ultimately arrive at happiness, but with each achievement I continued to ache in my ever-present misery.

While my life was one big Facebook highlight reel, I was falling apart bit by bit on the inside. I drank regularly and "Xanaxed" my way through work. My marriage was deteriorating and my children knew me as the mom who was always last to pick them up from daycare. I felt like a failure on all fronts, and my mental health was massively contributing to my inability to function at the last place where I looked like I had it all together: work.

Steeped in shame, I quietly hid from my co-workers, family and friends the huge pile of rubble my life had become. I was terrified of what people would think of me if they knew the bright shiny life I had created was a mirage of epic proportions. The weight of my eventual destruction finally became heavier than my ability to move forward. The one real option I had was to blow up my entire life by quitting the last thing I thought mattered to me: my job. The decision to leave my corporate job accounted for a costly loss of my identity, and without this identity, I could no longer make myself get out of bed the morning after my last day at work.

I was in crisis.

At the time, I thought my life was ruined forever. I know now I needed crisis to step in to show me the life that was meant for me. Crisis was the universe calling me back into existence.

This book is my redemption story, and my reason for writing it is just as much for you as it is for me. If you're reading this and you're going through a difficult time, I want to give you a place where you feel seen, heard and known. I want to share advice with you that can help you take action instead of staying in bed with the covers over your head.

If you are in crisis right now, action might seem like a foreign word to you. It's possible you're barely getting through each day. My form of action advice won't sound like traditional self-development books; I promise. When you are feeling broken, action might simply be taking a shower. When you start to feel inspired to make changes, action might be identifying your core priorities. Action will look different depending on each phase you are in now.

Speaking of phases, I have divided this book into three parts: Broken, Changed, Rearranged. These are the words I use to describe each phase of digging myself out of crisis. At any given point in life, I believe we are in one of these phases. Here's how I describe them:

- ***Broken:*** Sometimes the colors of our lives are like

winter: muted grays, dull whites and shadowy blacks. We are hard-pressed to understand our current circumstances and doubt the darkness will ever end. It's normal in this phase to wonder what will come next. When this phase goes on for too long, many of us experience sadness, frustration, withdrawal and depression.

While brokenness can come in the form of a crisis, I don't believe we experience this type of bottom regularly nor should we. In my story, I chose to share with you about crisis, but brokenness can visit us in less intense ways. Broken is the phase in which we experience the symptoms that tell us something in our lives is no longer working for us. This phase is about recognizing that something is broken. Perhaps our current job is draining our energy, or a close friendship has become more toxic than not, or we are giving too much of our time to things that do not contribute meaning to our lives.

If we allow ourselves to lean into this uncomfortable phase, we eventually will be inspired to start taking action. Allowing this "winter phase" to inspire our transformation is the catalyst for richer and more remarkable days. It prepares us for the beauty that will come next, which is change.

---

- **Changed:** Other times, life is lived through the colors of fall: rich maroons, bright oranges and vibrant yellows. As fall beckons change, it signals it is time to release the things in our life that no longer add to its beauty. While the broken phase was the indicator that a change was desperately needed, this phase is where we start taking action. In this changed phase, many of us experience renewed energy, glimmers of hope, and a willingness to try to do things differently than we had before.

Depending on your situation and where you're at, change will not look exactly the same for you. For me, the changes I made were more dramatic because I was digging myself out of crisis. My changes were focused on getting rid of the toxic truths I had accepted, which were contributing to my poor choices. For example, I began practicing saying "No" when people asked for something from me. There are many other changes I made that you'll learn about in future chapters.

For all of us in this phase, we work on clearing out old patterns, beliefs and ways of doing things that no longer serve us. It's about shedding things that no longer contribute positively to our lives. During this phase, we re-evaluate what we want and what we do not. Like the leaves of fall, we are letting things go. This magical season prepares us to make space to rearrange our lives in a more authentic way.

- ***Rearranged:*** Then, there are the times when you have put your life into such a brilliant new order, you see the world in the spring colors of whimsical teals, airy yellows and lively greens. You are enamored with all the growth around you and all the growth you created from within. In this phase, you will feel renewed, excited and joyful. This is not, however, a constant state of being—you are human after all.

In the rearranged phase, you are reaping the benefits of the hard work you have done. Perhaps you finally made a significant life change, such as pursuing a new career. Or perhaps, you finally put healthy boundaries in place with the friend who was constantly draining your energy. For me, this phase was more about rejoicing in the decisions I had made during my broken phase and the actions I had taken during my changed phase. Now, I was seeing and enjoying the growth in my life because of it.

In this phase, life feels authentic, free and beautiful. You have rearranged your life to reflect the truest version of who you are in this moment in time.

Now that we've covered the phases, I want to prepare you for how each chapter is divided. Each chapter in this book is broken into two parts:

———————————————❤———————————————

- ***Story:*** I share my own brutally honest and personal story about different phases of my evolution (broken, changed, rearranged). I do not hold back in these sections. The reason I am being my most authentic self when sharing my story is because I believe if I'm honest about my mess, it will invite you to be honest about your own mess. Too often, we think everyone else's lives are perfect. The reality is, no one's life is perfect. We are all messy, struggling and beautiful humans who are trying to figure out life. So, welcome to my mess. I hope it gives you the courage to be honest about yours.

- ***From Me to You:*** This is the section in each chapter where I put on my best-friend hat. It's the place where I offer advice to you about crisis, change and growth. This is where we have hot tea or red wine together in our pajamas, have a good ugly cry, and then figure out how we're going to move forward. This was the best-friend advice I desperately needed during all phases of my evolution.

Are you ready to dive into our story?

Let's start at one of my many new beginnings: I had a breakdown once, and it is one of the most terrible, yet remarkable, things that ever happened to me.

If you're feeling particularly brave today, I'd love to meet you in Chapter 1, where we can begin reclaiming our lives together.

Love,
Liesl

# Part I:
## Broken

*Sometimes the colors of our lives are like winter: muted grays, dull whites and shadowy blacks. We are hard-pressed to understand our current circumstances and doubt the darkness will ever end. It's normal in this phase to wonder when we will feel alive again. Oftentimes, survival is all we can manage, and it would be wise to accept that as a true accomplishment. This death prepares us for richer and more remarkable days. It prepares us for the beauty that will come next: change.*

# Chapter 1
## I Used to Rule the World

ne sweltering August afternoon in 2016, standing inside my cubicle on the last day of my job, I packed up what felt like my entire life into one small cardboard box. The contents included:

- Three outdated pictures of my two children in cheap craft-store frames
- A handful of self-development books
- A large vase that had sat on my work desk, serving as a collector of miscellaneous items
- Several ridiculous pens: most notably a heart-shaped monstrosity covered in gawdy red glitter

I reflected on the sad state of the box in front of me. It came across as both woefully underwhelming and surprisingly accurate.

Prior to the day I submitted my resignation, I was a human resources strategist at one of the largest global healthcare IT companies in the world. I was part of a select team constructed to focus on a highly visible project impacting the entire business. It certainly had seemed like an exceptional job.

So, how could the contents of my entire corporate career fit neatly inside one lowly box?

For this sixty-hour-a-week position, I had sacrificed everything that existed outside its walls, yet a great deal of glamour accompanied this martyrdom. Flying on the corporate jet, sipping cotton candy martinis in an MLS soccer suite with the CEO, and having our COO quote me during the annual executive forum in front of more than 1,000 people. These types of perks numbed me to the ever-present unhappiness that lived inside my chest.

My career did not stand alone amid a life based on a constant need for achievement. At a very young age, I crafted my ultimate to-do list, which I knew would lead me on the road to happiness. Like other perfectionist achievers, I checked off each neatly constructed milestone, except I used a glittery maroon pen to prove my superiority.

## My Life To-Do List:

- Marry the perfect man. At age twenty-four, I was married, marking the successful completion of my major adult-life Goal No. 1.
- Have adorable children. By the time I was twenty-seven, I had two children: one boy and one girl, only fifty-one weeks apart to the day. Take that life goals!

- Purchase a beautiful home. By the time I was thirty-two, my husband and I bought a $400,000 house in the suburbs, which was mostly my idea. I was confident we needed this house to push us to the next level of success. Plus, it allowed me to host parties and show off just how awesome we were to all our friends.
- Become an executive in the workplace. At thirty-four, I had a successful corporate human resources career and was on track to become an executive.

On social media, I was the person you loved to hate. I gushed about my terrific marriage and how complete my life was after meeting my husband. I filled our family calendar with several vacations each year and made sure you knew about each exotic locale. I gushed about how much I loved my job. I proliferated the unrealistic belief that you can have it all.

While making the virtual world jealous, I was certain I eventually would figure out the secret to what made for a meaningful life. I had begun discovering I was desperate for my insides to match my outsides. In the grandest form of misdirection, I hoped no one would notice I was one break-down away from full-blown crisis.

Back to the cubicle on the last day of my corporate career.

As I stared at this ordinary box and its contents, I became painfully aware it wasn't simply my career packed inside, it was my life. I had been convinced my corporate career would be the crown jewel in a series of achievements that promised the destination endpoint we all seek: true happiness.

Yet, there I was sitting crisscross applesauce on the dirty, lightly padded carpeted floor that belonged inside a sea of cubicles. I was emptier than I had ever been. I grabbed the sides of my pink leather Michael Kors shoes and hunched over the only remaining remnants of what I thought of as my entire life. I was anxiously trying to make sense of it all.

How had I fallen so far from the summit?

I had faithfully followed the crisply folded "Live Your Best Life" instructions the world crafted for my life; nonetheless, the final achievement on my Life To-Do List had failed to satiate the pervasive emptiness that lived inside me.

Was it really *my* to-do list to begin with?

As I tasted warm tears while deep inside my mind a voice I had once known well echoed: "Wasn't it supposed to be so much more than this?"

As crisis entered through stage right, the muffled sound of my teammates occupied the cubicle spaces behind me. Their voices became louder as I began to return to my body. They were fighting over who got to occupy my early-1990s desk chair and benefit from my oversized computer monitor.

I pretended to ignore their thoughtless banter while thinking, "Can't they see me sitting here – on the floor no less? Don't they know I'm falling apart?"

Realizing how insignificant I was to them, I began to return to the moment. I tried to press deeply into the events of the past few months that had landed me here, but it was harder than I thought.

During those final few months of my corporate life, time felt suspended, and the order of events were not neatly chronological in my mind. It was like flipping through the pages of a book in no particular order and someone quizzing me as to where each story belonged. Most memories are fuzzy mosaics in the background, pieced together by a collection of unique and unrecognizable parts.

My thoughts, feelings and body were in a form of autopilot that can only be described as putting your car in cruise control and deciding to take a nap.

With my mind flashing back through the events that brought me here, I find clarity. I suddenly knew which key moments of the past few months I needed to take away from this experience.

## Clarity Moment No. 1:

I am sitting across from my husband on the couch. He tells me he spent the afternoon in an emergency therapy session. Then he picks up my cell phone, which was resting on the arm of the couch, and says, "I recovered all your deleted text messages." I feel as though I've been punched in the gut.

He knows. I have been having an affair with someone at work. I don't remember the rest.

## Clarity Moment No. 2:

Sitting inside a fully transparent glass office with my manager, my palms are sweating as I hold tightly to the bottom of the chair. The anticipation of her knowing my darkest secret sits inside my chest, heavy, encased in butterflies and laced with fear. I search for what I will say if what I've been dreading to hear exits her mouth. For months, I had practiced this scene, but suddenly I have forgotten all my lines.

"It has been brought to my attention you are having an inappropriate relationship with someone at work," she says.

She knows.

Each time I had interacted with my manager since the affair, I was certain it would be the moment of my reckoning. I lived in a constant state of distress. Every meeting, every interaction and every glance was tortuous. My job became an invisible prison. Instead of an orange jumpsuit, I wore black pencil skirts, flowery silk blouses and layers of shame.

When this moment of reckoning arrived, it felt surprisingly like relief. My most embarrassing secret was now sitting between us. I no longer had any fight left. Instead of the denial-filled monologue I had rehearsed, I chose the truth.

Hitting rock bottom unites you with the truth of your story.

## Clarity Moment No. 3:

With the news now out at work, my husband and I decide I must resign from the corporate job where I had once imagined reaching the pinnacle of my achievements. We are planning our escape from this story. A decision that has led me here, to the floor of my workspace with my tiny cardboard box.

## Clarity Moment No. 4:

While three significant moments of clarity came to me while inside that cubicle as I prepared to walk away, I also knew I needed to remember this entire day. I needed to burn it into my memory as a reminder of how far you can fall.

What I most remember from that day is finding the clarity that had eluded me for so long.

Following this epiphany, I begin to return to my body. From inside my cubicle, I hear the sounds around me. I can feel my feet. I wiggle my toes. I hadn't realized it before, but my head hurts. I look around and life is still proceeding in the background of my existence.

The voice inside me is gentle, reaffirming and forceful. "It's time for you to leave. It's past time for you to go. There is nothing left for you here. Pick up that box containing the remnants of your career and walk out those doors."

I start to move. One of my colleagues notices and hurries over to walk me out the door. She hands me a lukewarm bottle of Kim Crawford sauvignon blanc and walks me to my car. "Your tags are expired," she says, then disappears from my life forever.

Numb, I sit inside my car for an hour trying to put it into drive.

Losing the identity I considered my crowning triumph with such a lack-luster sendoff is suffocating and painful.

I stare at the building for which I have sacrificed my actual life and real happiness.

Memories are flooding my mind. The late nights when I was the last person in the sea of cubicles working on a request from an executive. I prided myself on those late hours and for my IM always saying "Available."

Most nights, my husband would text me to ask if they should start eating dinner without me, and mechanically I would type back "Yes." Then, there were the vacations, during which I would be tethered to my phone answering e-mails and barely looking up at my children splashing in the swimming pool.

This building in front of me had consumed my every waking moment. And for what?

I had willingly martyred myself for a cause that slowly chiseled away at any source of joy that existed outside its walls. I had chosen this fate. Like most of my relationships, I had given too much. This love affair with work infiltrated my entire being in ways no others had. It rewarded my inability to say "No" with quick promotions, constant affirmation, and limitless opportunities. It fueled my unrelenting need to be the hero with heaps of praise for sacrificing my own needs to save the day.

It masked itself as the to-do item I needed to complete to attain happiness, but it revealed itself to be my own personal hell. This cycle of people-pleasing and achievement kept me locked in toxic patterns that eventually broke me entirely.

This building also reminded me of the deep shame of the affair, the mistake that ate away at my insides from the moment it began.

By the time I managed to drive away, I was an absolute wreck.

My marriage was falling apart, my children had not been a priority in years, and the one thing I had sacrificed all of it for had just flipped me off in the rearview mirror.

The weight of all my poor choices compounding started to manifest physically. The tension in my neck and back was sharp and immobilizing. I was completely exhausted physically and emotionally.

I screamed out loud in my car from a place of sheer loneliness.

"Does anyone care about me? Why doesn't anyone see me? I followed all the rules. How did I end up here?"

This was the moment my existential crisis invited herself into my life. I was broken.

Broken was a distressing heartache that released herself in between screaming cries and gasping breaths. Broken was the place where hurt, pain, sadness, bitterness and anger intersected. Broken was the most bottom place of my existence.

In hindsight, the pain she imparted was the beginning of a life I desperately needed.

A few weeks after I walked away from my corporate life, a realtor walked my family through a creamy yellow house with majestic white pillars. My husband and two small children discovered each corner with me like a game of hide-and-seek.

"This house would make a perfect inn," the realtor said.

We were a family in a vital search for a new narrative. We chose this one: Former corporate HR strategist leaves the sixty-plus-hour grind to open a charming inn nestled in historic downtown Lee's Summit, a suburb of Kansas City, Missouri.

I needed this story to save me because I did not know how to save myself.

## From Me to You

If you pick up this book, you know what it's like to feel broken. It's possible you are going through a difficult time right now and you are searching for something that makes you feel alive again. The thought of feeling alive might even seem like a foreign concept to you. It's possible you're so far removed from that feeling, you've told yourself feeling alive is reserved for other people. Your reality is heartsick pain. It is a deep pain you would do anything not to feel.

When I drove away from my job more than four years ago, I thought my life was completely over. I was certain nothing could feel as painful as the heartsickness of crisis. As I tried to put my car into drive that day, I was certain no one had ever hurt as badly as I was hurting.

When my co-workers were arguing over property rights to the items in my cubicle, I had given up all hope of ever being seen. I felt as though I was in the ocean drowning, screaming, and barely holding my head above water. They didn't even notice me.

One of the biggest lies I told myself during this time was that no one could understand me or what I was experiencing. While this sort of pain is all-consuming and lonely, I want you know you are not alone. In fact, I believe this is the biggest lie from which you must detach yourself so you can begin to get better.

While your experiences and stories are certainly yours alone, many people have been where you are. It's important to recognize the thoughts and feelings you are living through are part of a universal experience we all encounter in life: crisis, brokenness, heartache and pain.

What are the signs pointing to the fact you are going through a difficult season in your life?

## Here Are a Few of the Things I Noticed in Myself:

- **You often feel alone.** You might have convinced yourself no one really sees you. You walk through life wondering when someone will notice the deep pain inside you. It's possible your pain is so consuming you can't articulate what it feels like because it's a constant state of being. You believe your heartache is too severe to share with anyone and you can't imagine placing that burden on anyone. You need people desperately, but you find yourself isolating from others.

- **You can't identify what will help.** Even when people ask to help, you aren't sure what to say. The pain is too deep; it's too overwhelming to tackle. If you knew what would make it better, you'd do it. Text messages from people asking, "What can I do to help?" are well-intentioned, but you are too inundated to answer. The pain you are experiencing is all-consuming and the thought of any one action helping seems hopeless. This overwhelming feeling often leads to doing nothing.
- **You feel like even small steps are overwhelming.** You recognize the things you should be doing (such as getting out of bed, spending time with your family, getting to work on time, showering, paying bills, etc.), but even these basic tasks seem like too much to undertake. Your pain often distracts you from the things you should be doing. Even when you manage to focus on important tasks, your current state of reality sidetracks you. You desperately want to show up for life, but it's a challenge.
- **You feel as though the good parts of your life are gone and never coming back.** The pain you are experiencing is so deep, you've convinced yourself this is how the rest of your life will feel. Whatever you're going through seems permanent; you believe you will never recover from this moment. You've convinced yourself this new reality is the beginning of the rest of your life.

You might be able to spot yourself in my list. While it might not seem like it now, awareness is a beautiful revelation.

Before we continue, take a deep breath, a really good deep breath. Breathe through those tears. Embrace the awareness of where you are right now. Recognize you are seen, heard and loved even in your brokenness.

We are going to get through this together. Now, take my hand and accept the gift of awareness.

Whether you realize it or not, this is the beginning of your transformation story. This fall-on-your-face moment is meant to reveal the next version of who you are truly meant to be.

I want you to think about the most inspiring character you have come across in a movie or a book. Now, pinpoint the moments in which that character inspired you. While I can't get inside your head, I guarantee the character you picked didn't have an easy life. They weren't inspiring because everything was going their way. On the contrary, they likely overcame adversity and pushed through trials to deserve that place in your heart.

You might be broken, but this bottom moment is meant for you. Call on your courage. You must push through and not give up. I plan to be here every step of the way as we navigate through crisis together.

If you're feeling particularly brave, I'd love to meet you in Chapter 2, where we can begin our work on rising from the ashes. I'll tell you my story, and then you can whisper yours to me. I'll be there when you're ready and in your time.

# Chapter 2
## *Crisis*

---

The day after I drove away from my corporate life, I woke up at 10:00 a.m. This was approximately five hours later than when I usually popped out of bed.

The reality of the decision to quit my job sat inside my stomach as I fought back waves of nausea. I stretched, rubbed my eyes, and slowly regained consciousness.

As I shifted from dream world to the real world, I felt two distinct emotions: freedom and terror.

## Freedom was Quiet, Still, and Reassuring

*There are no more lies. The people who you love the most know the whole truth. The worst thing about you – the thing you kept safely hidden away – is out now. Inevitably, people will make their conclusions about you. They will choose to stay or choose to leave. Regardless of their choice, you are free from all the lies.*

## Terror was Anxious, Emotionally Guarded, and Loud

*Your entire life is over. Everything you've built is gone. Everyone around you will leave. Lie, hustle and deny. Do damage control. Play the victim. Blame as many people as possible for your poor decisions. Your parents didn't love you fully. Your husband didn't either. Your best friend convinced you this was a good idea. Make stuff up. Bury the truth so you look as innocent as possible.*

As freedom and terror battled for control, I contemplated what everyone at my former workplace was thinking about me now. I wondered if they saw right through me all along. I was fearful the truth of my life was on display for everyone to examine. I was certain everyone was talking about me.

Another horrifying thought popped into my head: What if they weren't thinking about me at all? What if my absence wasn't even felt? This notion was even more disheartening.

All this self-loathing brought on an apprehension. I quickly checked to see if I might be right. It was true: There were *zero* messages or notifications awaiting me on my phone.

Wait, there must be a mistake, some technical issue needing attention. I shut down the phone to fix the obvious glitch. When the screen popped back open, it confirmed what felt like an impossibility: Zero messages. Zero notifications.

How had I slept for more than twelve hours and yet not even one person needed something from me? How could this be?

There were no e-mails demanding immediate replies. There were no last-minute requests from executives who needed saving in the next thirty minutes. Not only that, but there were no children asking for breakfast, no permission slips to sign and no lunches to pack. My husband had left for work hours ago, apparently with the children in tow.

No one needed a single thing from me.

Soon, I became aware of a foreign sound: the sound of silence.

The sound of nothing reverberated throughout my bedroom. I didn't know what to do without the familiar fire drills that governed my life. The past three years at my corporate job had felt like a solid ten years—years ravaged by late-night demands, relentless weekend e-mails, and to-do lists that grew daily and were never completely checked off. They were the longest days packed into the shortest years.

Without the chaos to which I was accustomed, I did not know what to do or how to behave. Sitting alone in my bedroom was terrifying to me. I needed busyness and hustle to avoid facing the truth about my life. Silence required more of me than I could handle. I checked my phone again—nothing.

Begrudgingly surrendering, I uncomfortably tossed and turned until I finally landed in an uncomfortable resting position, trying to settle in: pillow behind my back, hands on my lap, and my gaze slightly toward the window.

The silence expected quite a bit of me. Silence required me to feel all the uncomfortable emotions I had been numbing for several months. Previously, anytime I was feeling an uncomfortable emotion like sadness, anxiousness, embarrassment or loneliness (you experience these often when you're having an affair), I would numb it. My numbing agents of choice were alcohol, Xanax, busyness and toxic positivity. I would regularly lie to myself by saying: My life is so great! I have it all figured out. I have everything.

This numbing of my uncomfortable emotions gave me temporary relief. However, a tricky thing happened once I started to numb too often; eventually, all my joy was numb, too. The world I lived in felt like one monotone color of gray. No contrast was provided in the vibrant colors that accompanied joy, happiness or gratitude. Being broken felt like seeing my world in a constant state of winter-muted grays, whites and blacks.

As I experienced the silence that morning, all the uneasy emotions I had suppressed for so long rushed to the surface. They were all jumbled together, rendering their parts unrecognizable. I didn't know how to pull them all apart and start naming them, so they manifested as one emotion: shame.

## Shame sounded like this:

*You are unworthy of love. No one will ever forgive you because of the destruction you have caused others. Everyone knows your secret and is judging you. You had everything and now you have nothing.*

Shame entered my life abruptly that day and told me I was utterly alone and completely unlovable. In that moment, shame tricked me into believing I was so wrecked that no one could possibly understand me. It whispered in my ear, "You can't tell anyone what you're going through. No one will understand, no one will sympathize. You are a burden. Sharing your story with anyone is too much."

I don't recall how long I sat with shame that day, but I had to snap out of it. I felt even more shameful wasting my day marinating in my own misery. I remember thinking, "My life isn't that bad. There are so many other people who have it way worse than I do. I should be grateful. I have a house, a family and people who love me. It's my inability to be grateful for this amazing life that has landed me here. I am clearly the problem."

My family would be home soon, and I did not want them to see me like this. They deserved the best from me. I had to figure out how to put myself together before they walked in the door.

Current-state Liesl had grossly chapped lips, red eyes, disheveled hair, and donned pajamas. As much as I needed to take a shower, I didn't know how to get out of bed.

"I just need someone to help me get up," I thought.

I could not bring myself to do the things I knew I should. Instead, I picked up my phone and started scrolling through social media. Mid-scroll, I noticed a post from a middle-school friend. She was celebrating an anniversary of her sobriety, and she had reposted an old blog from one of my favorite authors, Glennon Doyle[1].

The blog was a poignant letter written to people who were experiencing crisis. "I have been where you are this morning. I've lived through this day. This day when you wake up terrified. When you open your eyes, it hits you … the jig is up. When you lie paralyzed in bed and shake from the horrifying realization that life as you know it is over. Quickly you consider that perhaps that's okay because life as you know it totally blows. Even so, you can't get out of bed because the thing is that you don't know how."

1    Martin, Lauren. "Glennon Doyle's Letter to Fellow Recovering Alcoholics Will Heal Anyone Who is Struggling." *Momastary*. 5 December 2017, accessed 15 March 2021, https://wordsofwomen.com/glennon-doyles-letter-to-fellow-recovering-alcoholics-will-heal-anyone-who-is-struggling/.

Glennon Doyle's words interrupted my shame spiral. The truth wrapped inside her poetry made me feel seen. I no longer felt alone in that bedroom.

Inside her words, I located my pain. Through muffled cries, it felt as though she was holding my hand and whispering the truest most beautiful assurances into my ear. "You think this is the worst day of your life, but you are wrong. This is the best day of your life. Your angels are dancing. Because you have been offered freedom from the prison of secrets. You have been offered the gift of crisis."

I contemplated her words. Could crisis be the gift I was needing?

The affair had locked me inside a prison of secrets. I guarded the truth of my life from everyone, but I believed it was to protect them. I wanted to keep them safe.

With the secret of the affair now out in the world, it forced an honesty I could not have arrived at on my own. If I hadn't been so blatantly caught, I would have denied it to anyone and everyone. Despite my best efforts, I could not keep the worst part of my story locked away inside a prison of secrets.

The lock to the cell was opened the moment my husband recovered every text I had sent to my co-worker. The door to my prison was nudged open as I sat inside a translucent glass office and my manager said she knew. The door swung wide open when I texted back and forth with my sister about the affair and quitting my job.

I had served my sentence inside the caged prison of secrets, and now, my actual life outside those closed-in walls was about to begin.

On that hot, sticky August day following my corporate departure, the universe decided to send me a sign that it was time to step into the life that was meant for me. I was being asked to let go of all the lies, destructive patterns, and deceit that had landed me here. The universe reminded me I was not alone. I was not the only person who had ever been where I was now. I located my pain in the words of Glennon Doyle who had been in a prison of secrets and who not only survived but thrived. This prompted me to take the next right step: Get myself in the shower.

As the hot water hit my head, the shame and judgment subsided. While my life had been full of pain, lies and manipulation for quite some time, something higher called me to step into the life I was meant to live. In that moment, there was grace for all the choices that led me here. While the transformation that crisis promised me was still a thousand miles away, I was finally on the right path.

## From Me to You

If you have experienced that one awful day when you woke up and sensed your life was shattered, you might be feeling broken beyond repair. It might be impossible to simply get out of bed. You might feel shameful, unlovable and afraid. These are normal feelings.

Let me remind you, you are exactly where you are supposed to be at this moment in time. This story was written for you, and you have control as to how you respond. You have been given an opportunity to let go of your old life and begin living your new, better life. You might believe this is your breakdown, but I believe it is the beginning of your breakthrough.

However, you must invite that breakthrough into your life. Your reinvention will not happen if you do not take responsibility for your own healing. At this moment in time, you have two choices: You can stay stuck in the patterns that landed you in this story, or you can take a shower and start reinventing yourself.

## While you are trying to get out of bed, listen to the whispers of these truths that helped me get on the path toward reinvention:

- **Find voices that speak to you.** When you are going through a difficult time, it is normal to believe you are completely alone. There is a little voice inside your head who lies to you. It might tell you the pain you are experiencing is too much of a burden to put on anyone else. It makes you believe no one else has ever been this broken. In the extreme, this voice will make you feel crazy and hopeless. Entertaining this voice will guarantee you are stuck in bed forever. Let me assure you, you might feel alone but you are not alone.

  Pain is part of the human experience. While the social media highlight reel leads you to believe people are always happy and joyful, it is a liar. One of the keys to getting yourself out of this hole—and out of bed—is feeling seen and heard. It is knowing other people have been where you are, and they made it out. So, put down the phone and stop scrolling.

Instead, find the voices of those who help you feel seen and heard. For me, I started finding the truth I needed inside the words of Glennon Doyle. This evolved into finding other voices who spoke to me, such as Brené Brown, Jenn Hatmaker and Mel Robbins. I started following inspiring blogs and books, and I created a quote board to articulate my feelings. These were the voices who made me feel seen. Everyone has different voices who resonate with them.

Both my husband and my good friend Maki locate their feelings in song lyrics from the band Tool. Another one of my good friends, who was going through a divorce, began hosting Friday night dinners with recently separated women, which revealed to all of them that they were not alone in what they were going though.

Community is so important during this time. Even if you feel as though you've burned through your current community, make a new one. In the beginning, you might feel more comfortable with books, podcasts and following inspiring blogs. Whatever voices inspire you during this difficult time, fight to find them.

- **Focus on the step that's in front of you instead of the whole staircase**. When you are going through crisis, it's easy to become overwhelmed by everything you think you should accomplish. On most days, simply emptying the dishwasher feels like a significant chore. General life expectations can compound and feel heavy. You must lower your expectations regarding productivity, accomplishment and life goals. Do not compare yourself to others or even former versions of yourself. Instead, accept this truth: You are exactly where you are supposed to be. This part of your story might not be the one you prefer to read out loud; however, this chapter is as integral as all the others. Thriving in this chapter will look exceedingly different than other chapters in your life. I would argue it must.

Each day remember to focus on the step that's in front of you instead of the whole staircase. Focusing on the staircase will undoubtedly overwhelm you. The step is manageable (empty the dishwasher), but the staircase feels overwhelming (clean the entire house). Because I didn't know how to live in crisis, I learned to survive step by step. Your reinvention will happen slowly as you bravely journey up each stair. Accept that living your best life in crisis is still thriving.

Here is how I thrived living in crisis. When my alarm went off each morning, I'd asked myself: "What is the 'next right step' to take, Liesl?" I had two choices: stay in bed or get out of bed. Many mornings, I chose to get out of bed. After I got out of bed, I asked myself the same question, "Now, what is the 'next right step' to take, Liesl?" Take a shower or stand paralyzed in the bathroom? Most days, I chose to take a shower.

This simple question guided my every move: "What is the next right step to take?"

Some days, I did not choose the next right step, but increasingly I did. This simple question made it possible to wake up, shower, help my children get ready for school, and take out the trash. Some days, I even washed my hair.

On zero of these days would most people look at me and say, "Wow, Liesl is living her best life right now." *But I was living my best life.* My best life was putting together a series of steps that reminded me what it means to be alive.

- **Don't deny your difficult story or you will repeat it.** You must step outside the prison of secrets. The first step to being free of your cell is to stop denying your difficult story. You might not be ready to tell your story out loud, and that's okay. I know how hard it is to expose your truth. Most likely, you have been lying to yourself and the ones you love for some time. When you lie enough, the truth gets buried. You might have even started to believe your own lies. Those lies must be unraveled. You must stop believing all the fake narratives you have created. Denial, blame and lack of accountability landed you here. You are now called to something higher: truth, accountability and owning your story.

I used to sit inside my own head and blame everyone for my affair. My husband didn't love me the way I needed to be loved. My family life was occasionally dysfunctional. I had a "good friend" who supported all my bad choices. My boss was hard to please. And on and on.

I recognize we all carry around hardships that contribute to our poor choices. I am not diminishing the fact that many of our grievances are valid and truly felt. However, if you choose to spend hours ruminating about everyone who has contributed to your current situation, you will stay stuck there. You must focus on what you can control. You do have control of these actions: Taking accountability for your story, owning your mistakes and being responsible for your own healing. These are hard exercises, but once you accept the truth about your life, it will be considerably easier to move forward.

It's important for me to mention that I am not diminishing whatever traumas or difficulties you have experienced in your life. Those are contributing factors to the current story you have chosen. I am not asking you to "pull yourself up by your boot-straps and forget the trauma or hurt you've experienced." I spent an unmentionable number of hours in therapy working through my past trauma and pain. Your hurt is valid, but I am encouraging you to do the work and focus on what you can control. You have control over your own healing. You cannot expect everyone else to rise to the challenge of fixing your life for you. When your healing is contingent on someone else's actions, you have immediately given that person too much power.

*Please note:* This piece of advice is so critical to your reinvention, there is an entire chapter in this book dedicated to it.

• **Start feeling your emotions again**. Most likely, you've been numbing your feelings for some time. Numbing is something we all do to avoid facing negative feelings. We all have different ways we numb our emotions: food, shopping, alcohol, excessive travel, video games, busyness, etc. Start identifying your "go to" numbing behaviors. While most of these behaviors aren't bad in moderation, it's important to recognize when we are using them as escape mechanisms. Numbing behaviors are harder to pinpoint when the world around us sometimes glorifies and even encourages them. For instance, anyone could easily recognize that my overuse of anti-anxiety medication was a numbing behavior for me during crisis. However, the world applauded me for my other equally dangerous numbing behavior: constant busyness and hustle. The world perceived this numbing behavior as me "working hard to pursue my dreams and become an executive."

## I learned to recognize my numbing behaviors by asking myself two simple questions:

*Do I have control over this behavior? Or does this behavior have control over me?*

In crisis, it was easier for me to identify numbing behaviors. Several of my actions had control over me and were almost animalistic needs. I needed my booze, my Xanax and my busyness. When numbing behaviors become a part of your day-to-day existence, they are much harder to break.

For instance, after quitting my job, it felt impossible not to drink wine every day at 5:00 p.m. and mix it my anti-anxiety medication. I had to replace this habit by drinking sparkling water with lemon and sitting in a hot bubble bath. You may not be ready to feel your emotions. That's okay. Start by replacing one of your numbing habits with a healthy habit on which you can focus. In the beginning, I chose to focus on something less destructive to help me gradually ditch my numbing habits. I wasn't ready to feel quite yet.

Once you have successfully ditched your numbing habits, you can start facing your feelings. Everyone faces their feelings differently. I'm a writer, so naturally the written word helps me heal. I would journal my feelings because that was authentic to my own process. You must find the process that works for you. I have a friend who rides his bike for hours to process his emotions. One of my girlfriends spots her feelings in song lyrics. Discover an outlet authentic to you.

Naming emotions was challenging for me in the beginning. When I first started journaling my feelings, they seemed to fall into one of two buckets: happy or sad. I found it valuable to use the emotions wheel (Google that), which gave me more words to express what I was truly feeling. Naming and journaling my emotions helped me process them internally.

After finding the words to express how I was feeling, my list sounded something like this:

*I feel guilty for having an affair. I feel ashamed for letting my family down. I feel confused as to why I made the decisions I did. I feel helpless after making these choices. I feel anxious about what people think. I've felt alone for an awfully long time.*

These "I feel" statements were critical to stopping my shame spiral. Instead of believing I was a "bad person," I transitioned my thought pattern to "I made bad decisions." Successfully processing through your emotions will help you begin to navigate through this difficult time.

# Chapter 3
## *The Historic Browning*

♥

*S*ometimes amid living out our most difficult stories, something enters our lives that is meant to change our direction. It's as if the universe knows we are on a destructive path and an intervention is needed. I believe there is a divine portal that opens for a moment and serves as a gateway to remind us of what is good and true. It is the universe's last-ditch effort to call us back to the truest stories we are meant to live before it's too late.

Often, you can only understand the purpose of a story when you review it looking backward, which is why I'm telling it to you this way.

In the weeks before I left my corporate job, the universe opened a portal for me in an eleventh-hour effort to save me before it was too late. I'm going to take you back to that moment, which was two months before I packed up what had felt like my entire life into a small cardboard box.

Standing in our kitchen late one evening, I am lamenting, yet again, about my awful day at work. With our children finally in bed, I pour myself a full glass of white wine and the tears start flowing.

Bad days at work have become so commonplace that my husband, Harlen, mechanically grabs tissues from the Kleenex box before I can even think to reach for them. He sits down on one of the barstools behind the kitchen counter and locks eyes with me.

It is obvious he is tired and worn down. I am certain ninety percent of his exhaustion stems from my absolute unhappiness. Our lives are an absolute mess. I am wholly broken, but I'm not completely aware of this fact.

It is baffling to me that Harlen is even sitting in front of me. After coming clean to him about the affair a few weeks ago, coupled with the embarrassment of my boss finding out, I was convinced he would have left me by now. A part of me wished he would. My actions have been left unpunished, and now it seems too late to make reparations for the magnitude of these transgressions.

Once again, I am about to unload all the details of my bad day on him, but now there is an added layer of guilt. It feels unnatural sitting inches apart from each other. A relationship that had felt close, connected and healthy is now a remnant of the past. It's as though we are two strangers obligated to the vows that we spoke nearly ten years ago.

I wonder if either of us wants to be in this marriage.

To break the tension, I dive into the familiar cadence of describing the specific injustices of my workday. My voice is loud, dramatic and slightly overbearing. I'm in an out-of-body moment, hearing the words leaving my mouth and recognizing I have repeated these same lines many, many times before.

Typically, my husband would listen to me complain, validate what he heard, and remind me I deserve better. It was a standard pattern to which we safely clung. This time, however, he takes a drastically different approach. He is finally fed up. Instead of assuming a listening posture, Harlen takes control of the conversation as I am coming up for air mid-monologue.

In an attempt to get me to pull myself together, he says, "Seriously, we have this exact conversation at least twice a week. You say the same things you always do. You feel underappreciated. You don't feel like your boss sees everything you do for her. You feel overwhelmed by your workload, yet powerless to say *no*. This dialogue rehashes the same complaints wrapped inside a different story."

His boldness catches me off guard, and before I can retort, he continues.

"What do you want to do with your life, Liesl? If you could pick any career, what would you choose?"

What do I want to do with my life? I allow this question to sink in so I can develop an opinion and give an answer. Oddly, I find this question to be offensive considering our current situation. We have a family. We have a large mortgage payment. We have overpriced vacation habits. Moreover, I still need to achieve my goal of purchasing a lake house by the time I'm forty. His line of questioning is utterly unhelpful.

"You can't be serious," I say. "What do I want to do with my life? Is that a real question right now? You know what I want.

I want *you* to come up with some strategies to deal with our current situation. I want 'to-do' list hacks and a solid plan for being more efficient at doing everything for everyone. As a wife and mom, I don't get permission to have dreams. I don't get to imagine what I want to be when I grow up.

"Instead, I get up well before dawn to be on calls with India. I hustle to finish my projects at work and still I'm the last mom to pick up our kids at daycare. I spend the weekends folding laundry, preparing meals for the week and being selfless. I don't get to dream. I don't get to imagine anymore."

At this point, I am hysterical. He stares at me unsure what to do next. I grab my wine glass and summon Lily and Eugene, our two large Goldendoodles, to head upstairs with me. Harlen has been sleeping in the downstairs guest bedroom during all the turmoil and this is my signal to him I'm headed to bed.

Seething in bed for a solid hour, I self-righteously entertain the stupidity of his question. "What do you want to do with your life?" Seriously, his question is of no help at all. We have obligations we collectively built together. We must be practical.

Instead of pondering his question at all, I retrace each choice we have made together and take note of all our responsibilities.

## As I mentally inventory them in my head, the choices we had made seem permanent and binding:

- **A large house payment:** Staying in a modest house simply was not an option. Our friends were upgrading their lives and we followed suit. If they could afford to move on up, so could we. The executives at my company had pretentious homes in which to host parties, and many were buying weekend lake houses. Buying our big home would be the first step toward happiness.

- **House cleaners**: Once we moved into our new home, my workload was unmanageable. How else would we pay for our house without the income from my job? The only quality time we had with our children was during weekends. It would be ridiculous to waste our only free time cleaning a large house for half a day. Naturally, we hired house cleaners to do it for us.

- **Expensive vacations:** Everyone around us was traveling. They were taking their families on over-the-top Disney World trips and to sandy white beaches. Some of them were beginning to expose their children to international locales. We needed to get onboard and give our children a trip to Europe or perhaps Bali. I would not want their cultural exposure to be US-centric only.

- **Over-the-top neighborhood parties and gatherings:** Our neighborhood is one constant flow of social activity. There are always reasons to get together: holidays, birthdays, long weekends, Kansas City Royals baseball games, nice weather, Kansas City Chiefs football games and Hump Day. We are regularly hosting. It is not cheap to keep up with the Joneses.

This inventory of must-not-cut expenses appeared to be binding. But then, I take a second look. Are any of these choices really inescapable? Were they really my idea? Or was I influenced by the people around me who also ascribed to a belief system manufactured for us and not by us? More times than not, I was the instigator when deciding which material luxuries we had to have to be a perfect family. I know I was present for each one of these decisions and was a willing participate in arranging my life in this manner, yet they do not feel like my choices.

Now, that inner voice to whom I had stopped listening is saying, "What if you allowed yourself to imagine again? What if you stopped letting the outside world dictate your choices and instead asked yourself what *you* want? Did you want this large house? Did you even enjoy that Disney vacation your kids won't remember?"

This touches on the truth, but it is too much for me to handle in my confused and overwhelmed state.

I shut out these racing thoughts my husband has stirred with his illogical question and decide to marathon binge my favorite TV show, *Gilmore Girls*. Inside the small, fictional town of Stars Hollow, Connecticut, I am allowed to ask myself, "What makes me happy?"

## Here is the inventory I take during this reflective time:

- **Community:** In *Gilmore Girls*, when the entire population of Stars Hollow turns out for weekly meetings to discuss local festivals and weighty town decisions, they are part of something important. I am enamored with the small community events: parades, knit-a-thons, the annual winter carnival. I love how everyone knows one another.
- **Ownership and autonomy:** I appreciate the autonomy of *Gilmore Girls'* main character, Lorelai, who runs her own inn. She adjusts her schedule based on the things

that matter most to her. She is frequently working, but still makes time for her family. She feels pride and ownership in her business.

- **Love:** Lorelai and her partner, Luke, have a beautiful relationship. It isn't easy and there are only a few perfect moments, but they always express trust, mutual respect and loyalty.

As I begin to drift off to sleep around 1:00 a.m., I imagine how much simpler my life would be if I lived in Stars Hollow and ran an inn like Lorelai Gilmore.

While getting dressed for work the next morning, my husband's "unhelpful" questions are on my mind. Questions that seemed unreasonable to answer the night before, now have provided the clarity I needed and allowed me to imagine a different life, a different story.

Mid-thought, Harlen walks into the room to get clothes out of our large master closet. He notices me still there and turns around to head in the other direction. I walked into the closet to stop him from leaving.

"Harlen, wait. Can I talk with you?"

He turns around and looks at me slightly fearful, ready for Round 2 of the previous night's argument.

I surprise him, "Those questions you asked me last night really got me to thinking, and now I *know* what I want to do with my life. I *know* the career I would choose."

I take a deep breath and meet his gaze.

"I want to own an inn like Lorelai Gilmore . . . you know, from the TV show. I know how crazy that sounds, but I need something that only requires I take care of others. I want a place where I can help people rest and relax. Maybe I need that for myself, too."

Harlen smiles instantly, pulls me in close, smells my hair, and kisses me on my forehead. It's one of the first times we've touched in months. After which, he immediately went looking to make my impossible dream a reality.

In a rare instance of universe magic, it took Harlen only one Google search, one call to a realtor, and one conversation during which he convinced me to take a chance on a dream. He had found a historic property outside of Kansas City that could potentially be converted into an inn.

One week after our walk-in-closet conversation, our family of four is sitting in the long driveway of a large, single-family home in downtown Lee's Summit, Missouri. While we wait for the realtor to arrive, it's muggy and generally unpleasant, as a June day sometimes is in Missouri, where the weather is ninety degrees one day and snowing the next.

Sitting in our minivan, I am anxious and hot, so I grab the bottom of my flowy tank top and furiously fan it trying to cool myself and my calm my nerves. Harlen adjusts the air conditioning vents toward me and uncomfortably places his hand on my leg.

"Here it is," he says.

When I first glimpsed at the creamy yellow house with majestic white pillars, it was kismet. My gaze fixated on the back deck with a large white pergola, luscious green ferns, and adorable bistro tables. I give myself a moment to imagine.

In my mind, there are guests seated at every bistro table. I am wearing jeans, a t-shirt, an apron and ballet flats. My hands are full of warm cups of coffee. I am placing them in front of each guest asking if they would like any recommendations for their day plans. A couple with children asks me about the Farmers Market located down the street. I smile and tell them about all the available seasonal produce while grabbing them a reusable grocery tote to take on their journey.

Anticipating the possibility of my beautiful imaginary dreams becoming real, I am hopeful—and I am terrified.

## Hope was Quiet, Reassuring, and Loving

*This is the wrinkle in time that opens the door to the next chapter of your story. This is the place where you will feel the most alive.*

## Terror was Loud, Forceful, and Sure

*It would be selfish for you to take this opportunity. You have too many responsibilities to be pursuing this fairy tale. You must continue to give up the things that matter most to you personally to best love your family. Love is sacrifice. This dream is illogical. Turn the car around and go back home.*

Hope and terror still competing, the realtor finally arrives cuing my family to get out of our van. She walks us to the front door and points out the plaque on the right side of the porch.

"This home was owned by the Browning family," she says. "They owned a mercantile in downtown Lee's Summit. The home was built in 1889, and it is on the National Register of Historic Places."

She points to the two homes directly to the left of us.

"This is called Browning Row. When the Browning children grew up, they built the two homes next door so they could always live close to their childhood home and family. It's rumored those homes didn't have kitchens. Everyone came back to gather in this home for dinner."

She opens the front door and so begins the tour—and the beginning of new possibilities. Our two small children discover each corner and crook with us like a game of hide-and-seek. Though rarely at a loss for words, I am practically speechless as we move through the house. Each new room is further validation this home is meant for us.

"It would make the perfect inn. I know you don't want to live onsite, but there's even an extra bedroom for an onsite manager need be," says the realtor. "Also, it's located just two blocks from downtown Lee's Summit. There are so many shops, restaurants and numerous events in close proximity. Plus, there aren't any hospitality options this close to downtown. You would be the first."

She is right.

We are a family desperately in search of a new story and we collectively choose this one: Former corporate HR strategist leaves the sixty-plus-hour grind to open a charming inn in a suburb of Kansas City.

It is the first time in many years I allowed myself to dream.

After leaving the house, we walk two short blocks away to the town's annual Downtown Days festival. Our children get slushies from a shaved ice truck. Harlen and I munch on an overpriced funnel cake and sit in the green grass of a small park where a train station resides. In the shade of the large pine tree that serves as the Mayor's Holiday Tree each winter, we make plans to step into the story that has the promise of the second chance we crave.

On that blazing-hot summer day, I believe the universe opened a portal to serve as a gateway to the new beginning our family needed. As we sat in the shade, I was reminded even the most difficult stories can be redeemed. We merely must be brave enough to imagine, and then we must change direction.

## From Me to You

Have you ever felt as though you are living someone else's life? You are certain the choices that led you in this direction were your own. You remember each step and actively participating in organizing your story this way. Now, however, parts of the life you are living feel misdirected and inauthentic to your core.

It is possible you have asked yourself, "Wasn't it supposed to be more than this?"

Maybe you're so committed to this current reality, turning back seems beyond your reach. Perhaps you have struggled with truly understanding what brings you joy because you have been living for everyone but yourself.

A collection of choices now sits between you and the life you want. These choices did not happen at all once. They occurred subtly, one counterfeit choice at a time. Your life is now a collection of choices you don't recognize. Unraveling each choice now feels like an unattainable task. After living this way for too long, you've found yourself here, in the middle of crisis.

Which parts of your life led you to crisis and which parts will get you out? Separating the two might seem hardly worth your energy, but if you don't, you will end up back here or stay stuck here. If you retreat to your default mode of operating and persist in old patterns of numbing, you will be only temporarily saved from the discomfort of crisis. If you don't identify what it is you want exactly, you will find yourself at the bottom again—except next time, the bottom will be at the lowest depths.

How do you deeply reflect on what it is you want? How do you identify what led you to crisis and what will get you out of it?

## Here are two things that helped me:

- **Trust yourself:** Because a collection of inauthentic choices led you to crisis, a collection of true and authentic choices can certainly get you out. On the flip side, no one choice led you to crisis, so there is not one easy button out either.

  We often seek a life well lived via the thoughts, opinions and beliefs of others. We believe the key to living a meaningful life exists in the voices outside of us rather than the one within us. We accept truths that don't move us. We get married when we graduate college because that's what our parents did. We never question the faith in which we grew up even though it doesn't inspire us. We lose our entire identity after getting married and having children because the world told us mothers don't dream, they give.

  People often criticize the idea of trusting yourself. They think it leads to all kinds of terrible consequences. The foundation of the religion I once practiced thrived on this message: The devil wants us to trust ourselves because it is a sure path toward ruin. This belief made me terribly afraid of myself. I was certain anything that even dared tempt me to look at my own desires and needs was a one-way ticket to destruction. So, I locked that lady up and threw away the key. I became wholly selfless and decided my life was only to serve not to want.

Crisis completely changed the narrative for me.

Crisis taught me it is ludicrous to trust other people to define how I should live my life. The surest way I would hit rock bottom again would be to allow other people, religions, world beliefs and social norms to determine how I was going to live my life. I am not evil. There isn't anything fundamentally broken about me that requires fixing. I am not a damsel in distress desperately in need of saving. I am created in God's image. I am stunning because God is stunning. He created a beautiful voice that lives inside of me. He created one that lives inside of you as well.

Maybe the key to a life well lived is to stop searching for someone else to write your story for you. I believe your life will begin the moment you choose to write your own story. Maybe the person you've been searching for is you.

Listening to the voice inside of you can lead you on the road back to finding yourself. This voice reminds you of what you deeply care about. You simply need to recognize this true voice and begin listening. I believe this voice is still, quiet and reassuring. It knows the choices you need to make to stay healthy. When this voice speaks, it makes you feel light and safe. It illuminates the truths you need and not necessarily the ones you want. Your inner voice is not an enabler of all your choices and it certainly doesn't agree with your thoughts or actions all the time. People call this voice by many names: God, the universe, your inner voice. I call mine Truth North.

I heard my True North on the last day at my corporate job. She reminded me it was well past time for me to leave. I heard her in our minivan on a hot June day outside a home for sale when she challenged me to start imagining again. True North showed up the night I binged watched my favorite TV show and helped me identify the things that made me feel happy. She was with me inside a translucent glass office when the worst part of my life was made public. She reminded me to choose truth.

How do you begin to live a more authentic life? I believe the answer has been inside of you all along.

I found my inner voice in the quiet moments. She was the loudest when I muted all the noise around me. I found her in the hot bathtub where I closed my eyes and took in the silence around me. I located her in the early morning on my long walks alone. I found her on my deck when watching birds fly from branch to branch.

Recognizing the sound of your own True North will guide you toward living a meaningful life. Take note of when your inner voice is inspired. Notice the things that break her heart. Listen when she tells you something isn't quite right. Start noticing these moments and write down the emotions you are feeling, the physical sensations your body is experiencing, the beliefs that are stirring or the images being created about yourself and your world.

These collections of moments are the clues to a larger question you are asking yourself: How do I begin living a life that gets me out of crisis?

It happens one authentic choice at a time. You just need to listen.

- **Let go of your list of reasons "not to":** The answers you are looking for can be found if you're willing to let go of your reasons not to.

My list sounded like this: I don't deserve the life I want because I have responsibilities. I've made too many choices in the opposite direction of the life I want and turning back now is foolish. People will think I'm ridiculous if I buy an inn.

For a moment, allow yourself to let go of all the practical reasons you have constructed to not do what your inner voice is telling you to do. Allow yourself the opportunity to imagine. Allow the suspension of your current reality as you explore the next one. While I'm not encouraging you to be completely irresponsible and make destructive choices, I do believe the practical list we construct often isn't at all practical upon further inspection.

For instance, the reason I needed house cleaners every two weeks was because I was working sixty hours a week. I had zero time to clean because of my workload. Participating in every neighborhood party was not a real obligation; it just felt that way because I wanted to be included. Once I stopped hosting expensive gatherings, neighbors stopped inviting me to theirs. After my house cleaners stopped coming every two weeks, I cleaned the house myself with the abundance of time I had from not working sixty hours a week. The world moved forward.

Often your list of excuses for staying stuck inside crisis disguises itself as practicality. We believe the current life we've constructed (the one that led us to crisis) will not allow us to escape. In reality, we have more control than we realize.

I want to challenge you to explore your "reasons-not-to list" and examine it closely. Are your reasons indeed practical and logical? Or are they carefully crafted half-truths keeping you stuck in your current story? Can you make changes in your life to re-prioritize what truly matters?

## Chapter 4

# Own Your Story

*When we deny the story, it defines us. When we own the story, we can write a brave new ending.*
Brené Brown, professor and author

❤

A week after I left my corporate job, I was sitting across from my good friend Maki in a crowded bar and grill. She and I had been friends for several years. Our friendship began when our daughters were in preschool together and had become fast friends.

What began as an effort to get our girls together outside of school blossomed into a much deeper friendship between us. Maki and I connected over our similar family histories, our rather opposite personalities, and a friendship that developed organically. Eventually, our husbands established a strong bond as well and we got together as couples regularly. Throughout the years, our families became linked from almost every angle.

Even though Maki and I were close, I hid from her and everyone around me during the affair. Because I was certain Harlen had told her husband about what was going on in our lives, the urgency I felt to tell her grew each day. When I eventually mustered up enough courage to share my secret, I took the easy way out through a text message. I couldn't bear the thought of telling her in person. I was too embarrassed to face her.

However, Maki was not going to let me off the hook with a text-message exchange. She immediately called out my chicken approach for notifying her via text about blowing up my life. She returned my text with six words I dreaded reading, "Let's meet in person to talk."

Maki is someone who can see around corners. It is impossible to hide from her, and I was terrified to explain myself to her. After we arranged to meet in person at the neutral territory of a bar and grill, I felt vulnerable and exposed. It was unnerving to speculate about what she was thinking of me now, and I was frightened of discovering unfavorable opinions had been formulated.

While I had several acquaintances in my life, Maki was one of the few people for whom I cared most deeply. I wanted to keep her at all costs.

Prior to our meetup, I battled with an onslaught of emotions. I wasn't sure how many relationships would survive the mess I had created, but I needed her to be one of them. I decided the only way to keep her in my shrinking orbit of friends was to make myself look good. I desperately needed Maki to take my side. That day, I chose self-preservation over vulnerability.

To keep our friendship intact, I rehearsed my half-true story in front of the mirror several times. While I don't remember the totality of our discussion that day because I was emotionally fraught, I do know I painted myself as the ultimate victim in hopes she would pick me over Harlen.

As we ordered pizza and sipped on craft beers, I began my well-rehearsed monologue. At least half the stories I told were inarticulate and buried inside fragments of facts. The truth was harder to share than the lies I made up. If Maki rejected me based on the truth of my story, she was rejecting all of me, which was one of my deepest fears. But if she rejected the lies, this rejection would not feel directed at me personally.

The lies protected me from experiencing the vulnerability that accompany honoring the truth of my story out loud. If I shared the truth and she accepted me, real connections would ensue, but that wasn't the path I chose that day. I thought the lies were the key to salvaging our friendship, yet they left me emptier and lonelier as each line exited my mouth.

As I shared my "side of the story," I watched for nonverbal cues from my friend. As she usually does, she saw right through my facade . In the thick of chaos and half-truths, I forgot one critical fact about Maki: She has an uncanny ability to see beyond where people are.

Somehow, we had accumulated enough relationship capital during our years of friendship for her to sit quietly and listen to me without judgment. She could have eviscerated me with her words, but she chose to show me grace. I imagine it was frustrating for her to sit across from me seeing how broken I was and wanting to help fix everything for me.

Maki allowed me time to cry while I stumbled through my version of the story. Mostly, she listened to me that day. However, I vividly remember the one piece of advice she shared before wrapping up our two-hour session.

"You've been lying to yourself and others for too long," she said. "To begin getting healthy, you will have to stop lying to yourself. Then, you will be able to stop lying to others. You must start telling the truth and owning your story."

She hugged me, told me she loved me, and we parted in opposite directions.

Driving home that day, I contemplated the advice she had shared: Stop lying to yourself. Own your story.

These words kept running through my mind as I wrestled with what it truly meant to own your story. A part of me knew Maki was right, but the other part of me could not handle the emotional weight of owning my story. My story was so big and overwhelming. I wanted to stand outside of it so I could manipulate its parts and have control over who heard my story. I was afraid if I looked at it too long, this story eventually would own all of me.

## As I wrestled with the act of trying to own my story, a few things happened:

- Uncomfortable and upsetting emotions boiled to the surface. Telling the truth of my story made me feel shame, embarrassment, judgment and fear. I was ashamed the person I portrayed to the world was a huge fraud. I was used to being the golden child who people admired.
- A crippling fear of people judging me entered my thoughts. How would people respond when they knew my gushy social media highlight reel was a huge lie? What would they say about me when they realized my

entire life was a lie? Would they judge my story even more than I would?

- The anxiety of rejection was almost too much to bear. If I told the people I loved the worst thing about me, what would they think? Would they decide I was a horrible person? Would they deem me unlovable? Would they exit my life forever? What would they tell other people about me? I had no control over how others would react, which made it worse.

- Telling the truth made me feel out of control. Lying made me feel in control. Lying meant I could control the narrative and all its parts. I could create a story that made me look as innocent as possible. I could play the victim and potentially control the emotions of the people I loved. Control felt safer.

I contemplated what I would say to make me appear to be the victim: *My husband didn't really love me. He didn't give me the attention I needed. He never really saw me. He was part of the problem. He was the bad guy.*

While comparing the benefits and drawbacks between owning the truth of my story or lying, the most disturbing aspect of owning my truth popped into my head: What if I didn't even really know the truth? I had been lying for so long to my friends and family, the lies had become inextricably linked to my truth. I had lied so many times, I began to believe my own lies. How would I begin to pull apart the real parts from the fake parts?

I thought it was easier to abandon the hurt girl living this story. I did not think she was worth saving. I thought it was easier to abandon her and move on. My inner voice, however, fought with me regarding my perspective about this girl.

The voice I knew to be full of wisdom and truth whispered: *The girl inside that story is worthy of love. She is living out her hurt the only way she knows how. Grab her hand. This is only one story. It does not define her. But until you take her hand, you will continue to live out your hurt by damaging others.*

On that long drive home away from my friend and the bar and grill where I tried to escape my story, I decided to take Maki's advice. It was time to stop lying to myself and start owning my story.

My first step to owning my story started by grabbing the hand of the hurt little girl who was living out the toxic patterns and behaviors she had learned early in life. Instead of deeming her unlovable, I imagined whispering into her ear as she broke down at her office sitting on the gray floor under her cubicle preparing to exit it for the last time. "It's time for you to leave, I whisper. "It's past time for you to go. There is nothing left for you here."

## From Me to You

Some of us have stories we keep locked away. We hold onto these secrets tightly because we are fearful if the truth came out, we would be unworthy of the love for which we deeply long. The excruciating silence of secret keeping imprisons you, and one hallmark fear keeps you there: What will happen if the people I love learn my truth?

We believe certain chapters inside the book of our lives do not represent our most beautiful, best selves. Often, we hold firmly to the messy parts of our story because losing control of the narrative is too vulnerable. While I don't believe we should share the messy parts of our stories with just anyone, many of these untold stories block true connections with the people we love most who deserve the truth.

How do we overcome the fear, shame and pain often attached to owning our stories?

## Here are some things that helped me:

- **Accept that all beautiful stories are messy.**

  Has a character in a book or movie who lives the most positive, magical life all the time ever inspired you? Has a protagonist who drones on about their incredible life and how it gets better every single day ever moved you to tears?

  Nothing comes to mind?

  Of course not, because these types of movies and books were not created to stir us in any meaningful way. The stories that move us to tears involve hardships, adversity, and the will to overcome again and again. Would you have made it to Chapter 4 in my book if all I did was drone on about my perfect life?

  Being fully human encompasses experiencing every-thing life has to offer: Happiness, joy, excitement, pain, sadness, despair, loss. It means embracing each part of your story because it is part of what made you who you are today.

My ability to overcome crisis rested in the acceptance that my entire story was worthy. Each part of my story led me to back to myself and to my family. I am not proud of the story I chose. But without it, my redemption would not be possible.

When you start to feel shame about the messy parts of your story, remember that a meaningful life is not constructed of only your highlight-reel moments. Like the life of the inspirational protagonist in your favorite movie, your journey will—and should—include hardship. It is how you overcome hardship that makes you inspiring.

- **One single chapter in the book of your life does not solely define you.**

Right now, you might feel as though your messy story is all-consuming, but that's only because you are in the thick of it. You think a life well lived cannot possibly include this grim chapter. You are afraid if anyone knew the truth, it would make you unworthy of love and belonging. When shame seeps in, you might find yourself consumed with plotting ways to hide this story from yourself and others. It's possible you believe keeping this story locked away is the only way to keep yourself and your loved ones safe.

Before you abandon the person sitting inside this undesirable story, remind yourself this chapter does not fully define you. You are still writing the story of your life and this is but one moment in time. Instead of editing out the parts you don't like, recognize that owning your story is the key to your breakthrough. If you don't accept the truth, you will remain locked inside the prison of secrets constantly captive to your worst fear, "What happens when they find out?"

It is time for you to embrace this chapter in your life fully and to begin learning from it. It happened because it was meant to show you something about yourself that needs some work. Your breakdown can be your breakthrough, but you must accept every part of the story that landed you here. You might have made mistakes, but this story is *not* a mistake.

While this chapter in your life does not define you, it still has an impact on the people you love. You cannot experience true love and connection by editing it out. Although I am not a proponent of sharing your story with just anyone, you must share it with the people you have hurt. I had to accept the full truth of my story and share it with my husband. This was the only way for us to move forward. However, I want to caution you about something: You cannot move forward until you are honest with yourself first. Only then can you next be honest with the people you love. Your breakthrough is contingent upon these two steps.

This story is the beginning of your breakthrough. It has redemption written all over it. Own all the messy parts so you can begin living all the other beautiful chapters.

- **Get curious with yourself about why you chose this story.**

Accepting the truth of your story is the first step, but the work cannot end there. It is important for you to become curious as to why you chose this messy story. Like any good protagonist, true transformation only occurs when you are brave enough to uncover the reasons you made the choices you did.

If you do not take the time to discover the why of your story, you will continue to revisit and relive it until it teaches you what it is meant to. I believe each iteration only gets harder, so the sooner you understand the why of your story, the sooner you will move on to your next story.

For my entire life, I had lived out the patterns, beliefs and choices on a micro-level that eventually led me to an affair. My destructive decision to have an affair did not just happen; I'd been training for this story for years. Having low self-worth at an incredibly young age put me on the path to poor choices. Because I deemed myself unworthy, I needed people outside of myself to communicate my worthiness to me. While my inner voice fought for control, the voices outside of her were stronger. They said, "Don't trust your wants, wishes or desires. They are evil and so are you. You need something outside of yourself to define your worthiness for you."

I needed people to constantly tell me how great I was because I didn't believe it myself. I craved attention from anyone and everyone. I became what everyone else needed so I could get what I needed: attention. When a co-worker began showering me with the affection I craved, I caved to his advances. The writing already had been on the wall because I never addressed my own issues.

Addressing these issues was critical to my own healing. I had to identify why I chose this messy story. When I began this exercise, it was easy to play the blame game. Mine sounded like this: "The person I had an affair with had a personality disorder. I was the victim. I got caught in his web of deceit. It's not my fault. It's his fault."

While many of these statements are true, I am not a victim in my own story. I chose this messy story because I was living out my own toxic patterns. I chose this person because I had tragically low self-worth. I lived out emotional abuse cycles in most of my adult relationships. I learned love this way, so it was comfortable for me. As soon as I started working on my own issues, I gained back control.

Learning to honor my inner voice and making authentic choices led me to loving myself. Once I loved myself, I didn't tolerate toxic people in my life because I believed I deserved better. I stopped being the victim of toxic people because my strong self-worth did not allow for their presence in my life. I accepted there will always be people in this world waiting to take advantage of me. My perspective: I can't be taken advantage of when I simply don't allow it. These revelations were made possible only because I examined the reasons why I chose my messy story.

When you begin to examine your choices, don't make excuses. This isn't the time to blame others for your mistakes. Dwelling on how others contributed to your current reality will not help you move forward. Instead, take the time to focus on the series of choices that led you here. Again, I am not minimizing any trauma you have experienced in your life. In fact, I'm encouraging you to recognize your trauma, work through it with a licensed therapist if needed, and move forward.

Ask yourself important questions like: What beliefs about myself led me to make these decisions? What did I think was the benefit of these choices at the time? What emotions did I feel when making these decisions? What emotions did I feel after making these choices? What was the impact of the decisions I made?

Unraveling why you chose your story is challenging, but it's worthy work.

# Chapter 5
## *Pain*

♥

————————————————

*T*he weeks that followed my face-to-face with my friend Maki were spent wrestling with the truth of my story. The discomfort accompanying this exploration was hard to stomach. In the mornings, I stood in the shower trying to make sense of the heaviness I felt when revisiting my most recent choices. Uncovering the truth was only half of the exercise; facing the pain I caused myself and others was the other half.

The wreckage of my recent choices brought on physical and emotional pain that begged for any sort of outlet: crying, screaming, sleeping, feeling. I didn't know how to process the pain I had caused myself, my family and the other people I loved.

When healthy people experience the pain of owning their difficult stories, they take time to mourn and honor what their pain is trying to teach them. They experience healthy guilt for their actions, apologize to the people they have hurt and move forward through changed actions. At the time, I did not know how to do this.

The agony of owning my stories seemed too much to bear. Instead of revisiting my past to learn from my experiences, I dwelled in an unhealthy state. I got stuck inside the memory and overpowered with shame.

While I was still processing the fresh pain of crisis, I had little time to work through it. Instead, I had the huge responsibility of pursuing the next dream our family had chosen, opening the Historic Browning Inn. I had left my corporate job in August 2016, and we had bought the beautiful home we had toured, acting on what we had imagined was possible. Our target opening date for the home-turned-inn was set for November 2016.

A significant amount of work needed to be accomplished in four short months. We needed to build a website to take reservations, furnish the entire house, develop a social media platform, find an onsite manager, and develop local partnerships. Each hour of my day was carefully planned and filled to the brim. After which, I would return home to my family, cook dinner and run the bedtime routine. Rise. Repeat. Rise. Repeat.

In hindsight, this overzealous opening date was more about me avoiding the pain of my recent story to run to a new story. I had been cross training my entire life to avoid the pain of all my abandoned stories. My trusted antidote of choice was busyness. Busyness offered an artificial exit strategy from my pain. It was the lidocaine that numbed my truth. Unlike alcohol or prescription pills, the outside world rewarded my busyness.

This version of my new story was no different. Even while changing the narrative, I still used busyness as a diversion and jumped head-first into opening our inn. Throwing myself into this story distracted me from the wreckage of the last one.

When I ran into people I knew, naturally they would ask me about the departure from my former career. They would look at me with concern and politely ask, "Are you doing okay?"

Launching into my latest journey of owning my own business and operating an inn, I glossed over their concern. As I rattled on about my newfound entrepreneurial adventures, it sidetracked anyone from seeing the fresh pain from crisis I was lugging around with me.

This baggage was particularly heavy and unmanageable because it was part of a decades-long collection of unresolved issues. Hence, the need for an even more lavish and eloquent story than ever before. These conversations with people I knew ended the same way. I was praised for embracing a bold new venture, placed on a pedestal and admired by all.

Filling my emptiness with things to do was a classic Liesl move. If I did not stop moving, I did not have to feel anything. If I did not feel pain and shame, the crisis was not real. I needed to forget what happened and not let it creep back in. This led to filling my life with an over-abundance of new to-dos, coupled with a shiny romantic story that was the envy of all.

This defense mechanism had a deeper root I would later explore. At a very young age, I had developed a faulty belief that my value was based solely on what I did for others. Asking for help or being vulnerable was an admission that I was not valuable. I believed my goal in life was to serve others and sacrifice my own wants, wishes and needs. Being in pain made me vulnerable because it was an admission that I needed others to help me. My defense mechanism to survive my own pain was to ignore it.

While I was busy living out my new blue-ribbon dreams, I knew deep down sticking with this pattern was not working for me. While I filled my life with busyness, I still couldn't completely avoid the quiet moments that begged for my own self-awareness. In these moments, I was aware I needed to face the pain.

I wasn't 100 percent certain what facing my pain looked like, but I knew this hustle and bustle wasn't the answer.

Facing my pain didn't mean telling everyone how great my life was when I was actually broken. Facing my pain didn't sit inside remaining positive while moving forward into a new story. Facing my pain wouldn't happen by avoiding the hurt I had caused others.

It was time for me to stop running, but I didn't know how.

To figure it out, I returned to the voices of the people whom I believed knew my pain intimately. My original healers were not people I knew. Because I struggle with asking people for help, my healers were strangers. I read Brené Brown, Glennon Doyle, Oprah, Jen Hatmaker and Mel Robbins. Inside their stories of healing and redemption, they shared a unifying truth: Brave people who wrestle with their difficult stories feel their pain.

The stories of these women inspired me to stop running away from my pain and begin moving toward it. While pain is not comfortable, it is transformative when we permit ourselves to feel it. Leaning into the discomfort of pain allows it to pass so we can move on to the next chapter of our story.

I stopped running and gave myself the space I needed to begin to feel. While my days were jam-packed pursuing my entrepreneurial adventures and raising a family, I made time each morning for solitude. I needed this space to be fully present and to access the deep wisdom of my inner voice. Before anyone in my house woke up, I set aside an hour to feel my emotions without judgment. During the early hours of the day, I felt surprisingly vulnerable. As soon as my feet hit the scratchy builder's grade carpet in my bedroom, the truth of my story was fresh all over again. The mornings reminded me I really was not okay, and they provided a clarity each day from which I wanted to run.

In the first conscious moments of the day, I faced ever-present realities: You made a mistake, but you are not a mistake. The hurt and pain you have caused others can be redeemed if you are willing to do the work.

Creating quiet moments for myself was a big step for me.

Every morning, I would wake up early, grab the big box of Kleenex from the nightstand, make a hot cup of coffee, then sit on our living room couch with my two best dog friends at my feet. Once we were settled in, I would pull a blanket over my head, close my eyes, and try to sink into nothingness.

Being alone with myself was an exercise that was foreign to me. In the beginning, the solitude was grueling. I spent the time sobbing as I walked toward my pain and allowed myself to feel it.

Every now and then, Lily, my oversized, highly empathetic Goldendoodle, would jump up in my lap, plant sloppy kisses all over my face, then lay back down. The three of us would sit together for an hour. During this time, my dogs were my safest companions because they sat with me judgment-free. They didn't have opinions about what I should do to fix my hurt. They didn't point out the obvious errors I had made. In those early morning hours, we sat still together without critique.

This sacred healing ritual could last only for one hour each morning before the world required me to enter from stage right and repeat the rehearsed lines from the character I had created. There was breakfast to be made, backpacks to be packed and business plans to be executed. However, the real Liesl who emerged in the quiet moments slowly began replacing pieces of the fictious character.

Some days, sitting with my pain was excruciating. Other days, when the sobbing proved to be an insufficient outlet, I would scream into my pillow. Sometimes, it all became too much, and I would take out my phone and begin scrolling through social media. I would mindlessly review the highlight reels of people I had known in a former life. Everyone showed up here in awe-inspiring and poetic ways. I would wonder what the truth of their lives really looked like behind the happy photos and gushing tributes.

As I absorbed the stories of other people, I silently wondered if everyone else had figured out the secret to life, while here I was, balled up on the couch with crumpled, soggy Kleenexes in hand, doubting this debilitating pain would ever let up.

After a few weeks of sitting with my pain, it started to get easier. Eventually, I could sit for a solid hour without escaping to another distraction. The uncontrollable sobbing eventually turned into tears; the tears turned into sadness; the sadness turned into to peace and acceptance. I don't know exactly how long it took to process the pain from my crisis, but I am certain it was more than two full Kleenex boxes.

One October morning in 2016, I remember waking up to a crisp fall morning ready to start my quiet time. I made coffee, sat on our deck in a warm Sherpa blanket and prepared for the usual waterworks. They weren't forthcoming. On this morning, for the first time in months, I did not cry. Instead, I felt an unusual sense of relief; it washed over me not because my journey of healing was finished, but because something deep within me knew I had survived the worst part of crisis. I was still sitting here. I was still alive.

That morning, I went to Harlen's separate bedroom and woke him up. My presence surprised him. "Aren't you having your alone time?" he asked. "Are you okay?"

I looked up at him and said, "Yes, I'm okay. The hardest part is over. Will you just hold me?"

He tucked me underneath his arm and pulled me in close.

As I settled into this familiar position, I said, "I'm ready to tell you the truth about everything now."

Harlen took a deep breath in, then exhaled. "I'm ready."

Our marriage started down a healing path that morning. I told him about facing my pain and accepting the truth of my story. I shared with him the things I learned in the quiet moments when I wrestled with the lies, the denial, the anger and the hurt. I told him my story out loud, and then he told me his. Some parts felt like two different narratives viewed through our separate lenses. I didn't question his view of reality and he didn't question mine. He cried and I cried, but we never moved away from each other. While we faced our collective pain together, we took a few tiny steps toward each other. It was the first time in months I felt close to him.

In the quiet morning moments of October 2016, I said good-bye to the worst part of crisis. The past few months before then had been spent owning the truth of my story, facing my pain, and choosing the authenticity my inner voice pushed me toward. Now, I was ready to begin repairing my marriage, my family and my life.

## From Me to You

One of the biggest lies we buy into is that we should do everything possible to avoid pain and sadness. Instead of experiencing the full spectrum of our emotions, especially the undesirable states of being, we should singularly chase the duo of joyfulness and happiness.

We place a higher premium on blissful, harmonious emotions because they create euphoria. Feelings of joyfulness and happiness often occur during the crescendo moments in our lives. They are the end-product of working through less pleasant states of being. They are part of the highlight-reel moments of our lives.

Certainly, these euphoric moments are worthy of attaining and sometimes sustaining in parts of your life, but it is unrealistic for this to be your constant state of being. No human can possibly attain happiness 24/7, unless they are living in a massive state of denial.

Yet, the social media highlight reel seems to convince us otherwise. We are bombarded daily with people's exhilarating moments. What was once an annual holiday card from a handful of actual friends showcasing a special family memory or two has transitioned into a constant stream of happy highlights from people who generally are strangers to us. Our brain cannot process access to 1,000-plus people and their perfect Instagram-worthy moments.

Based on what we see second-hand, we assume everyone we know must be living in a perpetual state of happiness—and we have a need for them to think we are living the high life, too.

These only-on-social-media fantasy lives confuse our emotional resilience when we experience true hardship. Because our society reinforces the value of happy feelings, we believe something is wrong with us when we experience the full range of real-life emotions. Instead of being emotionally curious as to why we're so sad, we stuff those feelings down and numb them with the temporary happiness hacks sold to us: lavish vacations, expensive wines, luxury shopping, 24/7 busyness, prescription pills, toxic positivity, denial. Not of all these things are bad for us, but they are when we start using them as escape mechanisms.

When real life happens, we are not good at dealing with anything that forces us to encounter discomfort. Inevitably, there are moments that invite sadness, pain and suffering into our lives. Some of these situations we can control, but many we cannot, such as a global pandemic, a cancer diagnosis, our spouse's affair, a divorce, a midlife crisis or the loss of a child. We must observe, feel and move through the pain and despair of these situations.

This is not to suggest we should sit inside our pain permanently and camp out there. Completely avoiding pain and discomfort can be similarly destructive. Pain is an equal teacher to joy. I am not the first person to communicate this truth.

Pain, sadness and despair are signals that we need to get curious about our emotions. Instead of cozying up on the couch and drinking five glasses of wine while watching *The Bachelorette* (never done that; clearly not a personal example), I want to challenge you to be brave. All emotions are data points. Instead of trying to reshape the less pleasant ones into something positive, I encourage you to sit with them for a while.

How do we sit with our pain and allow it to transform us? **Here are some things that helped me:**

- **Change what you believe about pain.**

  While pain is uncomfortable, it is part of the human experience. Every person will go through painful moments at some point in their lives. Might I remind you that you have survived every moment leading up to this one. This moment is no different. You are far more resilient than you give yourself credit.

  Remember your favorite book and movie characters? Those characters inspired you because of how they faced their hardships and pain. They walked through them and came out better on the other side What they did with that pain is what makes them exceptional.

  Instead of viewing your pain as a moment in time, see it as the end-product that brings transformation. If you allow your pain to teach you something, it eventually will become your power. When you are in the middle of sorting through your hurt, be encouraged that joy will visit you again. Feeling your pain is a rather remarkable part of being human.

Running toward my pain in the quiet moments of the morning was a game-changer. It wasn't pleasant, but it was a wise teacher. Bravely facing the pain I caused myself and others allowed me to experience real remorse. Permitting myself to feel gave me insight into the hurt I had caused others. When I faced my pain, I recognized I was a hurt woman who couldn't help but hurt others. Pain is a wise teacher. If you can reframe your beliefs about pain, it promises transformation.

• **Carve out time to be alone and process your emotions.**

Our lives have many distractions baked into them. It's important to find uninterrupted time each day to sit still in quiet and process your pain, allowing yourself to feel it.

*Start small.* In hindsight, an entire hour of sitting with my pain—especially for a pain-sitting novice—was too much. Consider ten-minute increments. During this time, ask yourself important questions, such as:

What am I experiencing in this moment? Crying, tightness in my neck, a feeling in my chest?

Can I name the emotions I am feeling? Sadness, despair, mournfulness, anger, frustration, anxiety, irritation?

Can I accept the truths about my pain without judgment? Do not say: I have a great life. I shouldn't feel this way. There are people who have it much worse than I do. There will always be people who have it worse than you. This is an excuse for minimizing your lived experiences and it will not help you deal with your own issues.

- **Learn from your pain.**

  After you have processed your emotions, don't forget to focus on the lesson. Take the time you need to gather insight from your experiences. An important note: Do not spend too much time dwelling on your pain.

  While it is important to feel pain, you also must let it pass. It won't help you to ruminate on it for too long. The purpose of pain is for it to be felt, for it to teach you something important, and for it to ultimately transform you.

  For me, learning from my pain meant revisiting the most bottom place of my existence. I allowed myself to experience the heartache associated with pain and it became a great teacher. Facing my own pain taught me the importance of talking to my husband, children, family and friends about the hurt I caused them during the affair. Because I felt my own pain, I knew it was right to invite others to share openly about the pain I caused them. It revealed the importance of apologizing for my many mistakes and crying with them. Pain is the birthplace of redemption. If we allow it into our lives, it can transform us into the next version of who we are meant to be.

# Chapter 6
## Crisis-Proof Friendships

---
♥
---

It is late October 2016, and I am sitting on the hardwood floor in the master bedroom inside the Historic Browning Inn. I am alone on this Tuesday afternoon, as my family is away attending to their work and school obligations. I am furiously painting the baseboards in a fresh coat of white paint.

We are three short weeks away from opening day, and it's crunch time. The growing to-do list is all consuming. My family is singularly focused on one objective: open the inn by mid-November in time for our first reservations. To make this happen, no task—no matter how big or small—is beneath us.

I can't remember picking up a paint brush at any point in my life, but I quickly learn entrepreneurship requires I regularly fill in the gaps. On that Tuesday afternoon, I have traded in my standard corporate uniform of black pencil skirts and silk blouses for ratty black yoga pants and old t-shirts. My hands and arms are covered in white paint.

Never in my wildest dreams did I imagine my day job would include anything that resembled manual labor. Yet, the quiet, monotonous movements of painting feel oddly fulfilling and slightly therapeutic. As I listen to my Spotify list and focus on the task at hand, it is the first time I realize the inn possesses a calming and healing energy. When I am at the inn, my inner voice feels as though she is front and center. The energy of the home has given her a microphone, and I am her captive audience.

A week prior, my brother-in-law Jack made a special trip all the way from Minnesota to Missouri to help us prepare for the opening of The Browning. Thankfully, Jack is a professional painter, and he spent an entire week covering every square inch of the inn's walls in a cool owl gray. The color freshened up the space and augmented the tranquil feeling.

During Jack's four-day marathon painting session of the large home, there was no time to address the baseboards. Considering my magnanimous task list, Harlen urged me to leave the baseboards unpainted. Being the perfectionist I am, I simply could not let it go; it had to be done.

In mid-October, we had officially closed on the Historic Browning Inn and had reservations scheduled in November. Our first reservation was an infinitely trusting wedding party who had not even seen the space when they booked with us. Unlike many inns, our family was not living in the home. We often joked no one would covet a vacation with two large dogs and two small children.

With us not living at The Browning, it had absolutely no furniture, no kitchen items, no appliances, no beds and none of a dozen other necessities. Furnishing a 3,000-square-foot home was no minor task, and there were still several other items to check off the list before opening day.

When I originally committed to the mid-November timeline, it seemed entirely realistic. Per usual, I was overzealous in my estimation. The amount of work to be completed was significant, and even my master project plan couldn't save us from numerous unanticipated challenges. It was far too much for our family to take on alone. Yet, we persisted.

During the day, my husband was working a more-than-full-time job and my children were in school. My days alone at The Browning were spent trying to check items off the ever-growing to-do list. The constant busyness of getting ready to open our historic inn was coupled with the freshness of working through crisis. Most evenings were spent at the Historic Browning hanging pictures, repairing walls, painting furniture, cleaning windows and eating takeout on the floor. When we finally would return home, our children went to bed way too late every night and our family ran on fumes for longer than I care to admit.

Our family needed help; *we* had taken on too much. Although, if I am being brutally honest, *I* had taken on too much and everyone else was helping carry this tremendous weight. As I've admitted, I have a tough time asking for help. Needing things from people makes me feel vulnerable, so I place my value on being self-sufficient. Even the smallest asks for help feel as though I am putting an undue burden on others. My identity had been rooted in being the helper, not the person needing help.

During my crisis, my inability to seek support was heightened because it was coupled with my shame. I was embarrassed that the truth of my story was on public display for our friends and acquaintances, rendering me even more un-helpable than before. I was certain Harlen was the hero of our sordid story, which left me playing the role of the epic failure in our lives. Asking my brother-in-law to travel hundreds of miles to help us paint The Browning was arduous enough for me; seeking out anyone else's help seemed rude.

I was convinced everyone who mattered to us would exit our lives anyway.

This self-fulfilling prophecy was partially true. Plenty of people walked out of our lives during crisis. My husband affectionately gave them a title: "good-time friends." These good-time friends enjoyed our company when our lives seemed impressive. They wanted to have patio drinks once a week, attend our over-the-top parties and be around us when everything was going smoothly. But when our lives fell apart, these people quickly exited stage right. These connections were superficial and built on alcohol, gossip and "good times."

After crisis hit, the invitations from good-time friends were no longer forthcoming; instead, stories were created about our family and we were unceremoniously discarded. At the time, it felt unforgivably hurtful and reinforced my fear that I was unlovable and beyond help. During this time, my vision was immensely short-sided, as I was exceedingly focused on being everyone's "friend." Looking back, being forced to remove these insincere connections from our lives created space for meaningful connections. Our circle may have gotten smaller, but it was mightier.

The people who showed up for us in crisis disproved all the beliefs I carried around about myself. Most of these people knew our family was broken and were well-acquainted with our story. During this period when I had a hard time simply getting up each morning, these people started showing up for us and offering to help without my prompting.

My good friend Melissa, who owns a boutique in downtown Lee's Summit, Missouri, took on the tremendous responsibility of furnishing and decorating the Historic Browning. She spent many evenings and weekends picking out items to make the inn inviting. Her daughter, Amanda, inhabited the inn's garage nightly for more than a week repainting furniture and reupholstering chairs.

One Saturday, a group of friends showed up at the inn to clean windows, rake leaves and paint trim. My dear friend Maki and my sister, Marta, called regularly for progress updates and listened to me talk about moving into the next part of the story we were creating. My good friend Jodi went on long walks with me regularly as I worked through the hardest part of my story.

These were the "crisis-proof friends." It is likely many of these crisis-proof friends didn't know exactly how to help me during this seemingly impossible period in my life. I am sure many of them fumbled for the right words to say to me, and I am certain every single one of them had better things to do with their time. Most of them never spoke a word about the crisis at hand unless I brought it up first. They didn't ask me how I was doing with concerned eyes or judgmental looks. I never felt pitied even once from these true friends.

In August 2016, I felt as though my life was finished. End of story. Getting out of bed was a daily struggle. I was certain once people discovered the worst part of my story, they would exit my life forever. From my viewpoint, I had failed miserably at life. I believed I was unlovable, unworthy, broken and shameful.

No longer could I perform or lie my way out of the mess I had created. Instead, I willingly accepted defeat. I brought no value to the people I loved. With no relationship capital exchange, I could be easily discarded. Even if I were able to put all my broken pieces back together, I believed I would need to seek out new people to love me. I didn't think it was possible for anyone to love me through the truth of my story.

By October 2016, a small group of my friends and family decided to invalidate the stories I had been telling myself since I was a young girl: You must hustle for your own worthiness. Your worthiness lies in the value you bring to others. If you do not bring value to others, you will be discarded.

This core group of people showed me what it looked like to sit with someone inside their pain. They showed me how real love felt. During this excruciating time, these individuals didn't ask me what I needed. I think they recognized even I didn't know what I needed. Instead, they started guessing for me. They showed up with hammers, paint brushes, cups of coffee, late-night phone calls and long walks that were all about me.

These people loved me when I was still figuring out how to love myself. They showed me that real love was not only about showing up for you when you're at your best, but it also is about showing up for you when you're at your worst. They were a small group of angels, but they were mighty.

Unknowingly, they assembled the next dream our family needed to heal. Their actions were a quiet whisper that said,

"I see you. I do not completely understand this load you are carrying on your back, but for a few moments, we will carry it together."

## From Me to You

Crisis has a way of uncovering the people who really matter in your life. When you are going through a difficult time, you will lose people and connections. These losses will be distressing, and you will feel hurt, which is understandable. Take the time you need to grieve.

From my perspective, however, fixating for too long on the loss of certain connections will waste the limited energy you have. I spent far too many nights obsessing about what people were saying about me and wondering why all the invitations had stopped rolling in. Spending too much time mulling over these losses will only make you feel more broken. Accept that not every person you meet is meant to hold space for you during a difficult time. Instead, turn your attention to the people who are showing up for you.

## Here are some observations that helped me find perspective during my difficult time:

- **Not everyone is talking about you.**

  When your world is falling part, it is all consuming. When I was in crisis, I believed people were focused on my downfall. The reality was, most people were not paying that much attention. The amount of time I spent replaying in my mind what other people might be saying about me was a waste of time.

Case in point: I asked a close friend and executive at the company where I had formerly worked what everyone said about me after my departure. She did not remember people talking about me at all. People went about their regularly scheduled programming, got their Starbucks coffee in the café downstairs and delivered on the company objectives. I had agonized daily about what they might be whispering about me. What had it accomplished? Nothing except zapping my energy and gobbling up my time.

Whenever I found myself caught up thinking about what others might be saying about me, I would change my focus to what my crisis-proof friends were saying about me. They were the people whose opinions mattered.

My crisis-proof friends sounded like this:

*You made a mistake. This moment does not define your entire life.*

*You need to surround yourself with people who love you during this time.*

*Your comeback is going to be pretty legit.*

- **Not all good-time friends can become crisis-proof friends.**

I used to believe the people who exited my life during crisis were mean and vindictive. I thought they were trying to intentionally hurt and exclude me. It was painful to drive by my neighbors' homes and see an assembly of the neighborhood group to which I had once belonged having patio drinks without us. The reality was, we simply had not built strong enough friendships or relationship capital to survive crisis.

My good-time relationships were built on Kansas City Royals watch parties, *The Bachelorette* marathons, gossip about who needed to paint their garage and more wine than was necessary. These types of interactions did not build a solid foundation for surviving difficult times.

It's not unhealthy to maintain some good-time friendships, and I'm not trying to villainize these friends. In fact, it's important to hold space for several of these surface-level connections. Everyone needs neighborhood friends they can invite over for Halloween or trade cookies with during the holidays. Not every friendship you invest in needs to be deep and meaningful—you wouldn't have the time for it anyway. It is important, however, not to mistake good-time friends for crisis-proof friends. You will be disappointed if you expect good-time friends to be there for you when times get tough.

Another mistake that is easy to make is not having a good balance of both types of friends. Prior to going through my crisis, I had a strong desire for everyone to like me. Because I was spread so thin and didn't have the time to invest in each of these relationships, most of my friends became good-time friends. Personally, I have learned the balance of good-time friends and crisis-proof friends is necessary and important. When a difficult time hits, you will be thankful for the loyalty and investment you made with your crisis-proof friends.

- **Crisis will reveal who matters.**

The people who show up for you during a difficult time are your people. The people who loved our family at its worst gained my captive and loyal attention. There were not many of them, but their presence was noted.

Crisis-proof friendships typically do not come in large numbers because most people do not have the capacity to hold space for more than a few of these deeper relationships. These friendships are carefully curated and built over time. They are based on a series of moments, events and conversations that cultivate longer-term trust and intimacy.

Outside of my family, I have only four crisis-proof friendships: Maki, Jodi and two Melissas. When I am faced with the choice of whom to invest in, these four women always come first. They are my "drop-every-thing-for" people. If they need me, I will drop pretty much anything else I am balancing to be there for them. Even if it's something as minor as one of them is hosting a get-together that conflicts with another invitation. I will choose them every time.

If they need me to update their resume using my Human Resources skills, I'm available tomorrow. If they are sick and can't get to the grocery store, I'm sending a grocery delivery with all their favorite snacks. If I prioritized all my friendships this way, I would be pulled in a thousand different directions. It is impossible to be everything to everyone without burning out. Crisis-proof friends are a small circle of people, and they are the relationships where you should invest much of your time. I check in with the four women in my crisis-proof circle at least once a week via voice text, handwritten note, or scheduling a get-together.

Crisis will reveal your good-time friends and your crisis-proof friends. While you will lose friends during hard times, I would argue you are losing the people you need to so you can focus on the people who matter most. You will have made room in your life for the people who truly care about your well-being. The truest loves of your life will embrace every part of you: the good, the bad, the beautiful and the ugly. Instead of focusing on the friendships you have lost during crisis, focus on the true friends you have gained.

Channel your limited emotional energy into these people instead of focusing on the good-time friends who are excluding you from the party down the street. Whenever you have available energy, text, call and set up coffees with your crisis-proof friends.

## One More Suggestion

While your path will cross with many good-time friends, don't ever forget about the people who showed up for you during your dark night of the soul. They are precious. When the good times come again (and they will come again), your good-time friend pool will inevitably grow as a result. Rejoice in the good times, but do not ever forget to prioritize the truest loves of your life.

Choose them over all others. Fight for them. They have revealed to you that loyalty, deep connection and love is about sitting with people inside their pain. They were your angels who reminded you that you were worthy even when you couldn't see it yourself.

# Chapter 7
## *Real*

---💙---

It's early November 2016, and I am returning home from a particularly long day at the Historic Browning Inn. Most of the day was spent painting the ugly green subway tile in the kitchen to a transformative eggshell white. The rest of the day was consumed with scrubbing baseboards with bleach and finding a photographer to take pictures of the rooms for our website.

My good friend Melissa, the owner of a boutique, spent most of her day decorating the inn. Part of the décor transformation included identifying walls that needed mirrors, pictures and art. Melissa had carefully laid the complimentary items against each wall in the house and penciled in the exact location where each piece would be hung.

I am dreading returning home and telling Harlen I need him to return to The Browning that evening to finish the picture-hanging task. There have been so many late nights for us recently, and he's been working double with his full-time job and helping me with the business. To preemptively make peace prior to unveiling an additional to-do item, I grab our family dinner from our favorite local pizzeria on my way home.

As I walk into the house, I immediately notice our seven-year-old daughter, Mady, balled up on the couch with tears in her eyes. I set the food on the counter and Harlen grabs a stack of paper plates from the pantry. As we arrange dinner on the counter together, my husband says, "She had a bad day. Some of the girls at school were making fun of her."

While I hardly have enough energy to shove food into my mouth and manage to crawl into bed, I know Mady needs me. My absence in my daughter's life these past few months during my crisis is apparent to me as I search my memory for the last time we had a heart-to-heart talk. I motion Harlen to finish setting up dinner as I make my way to Mady on the couch.

I kneel next to her, touch her hair, and say, "Hello, my little penguin (my endearing nickname for her). What happened today?"

Mady manages to look up at me for a moment and says, "The girls were making fun of me at school."

"Would you like to talk about it?"

"No. I just want to eat."

Mady is quiet and introverted. I've learned it takes time for her to process her emotions internally before she's ready to talk. So, I respect her space and call everyone to dinner. As we are eating, I break the news to Harlen about hanging the pictures at The Browning. I know he's exhausted and unhappy with my request, but knowing we have an impending deadline to meet, he obliges.

After cleaning up from dinner, Harlen says he's going to change out of his work clothes and get ready to head to the inn. It's getting close to the kiddos' bedtime, so I'll run the bedtime routine while Harlen runs to complete yet another to-do at our new dream.

Harlen heads out the door with his toolbox in hand. Mady and our six-year-old son, Ethan, respectively take their showers, brush their teeth and get ready for bed. Mady emerges from her bathroom wearing her fuzzy penguin pajama pants and carrying her well-loved plush penguin named Chinny.

She looks up at me with tears in her eyes and says, "Mom, can I sleep with you tonight?"

It has been a while since she's asked, so I willingly oblige. I pull back the covers, tuck her in and head to Ethan's room to kiss him goodnight. After finishing the bedtime ritual with Ethan, I crawl into bed next to Mady. As I reach over to kiss her goodnight, she has one additional request, "Mom, can we listen to a story?"

Whenever Mady endures a particularly bad day, she likes to crawl into our oversized bed with her constant companion Chinny and listen to her favorite stories via audio. This ritual has been absent from our lives for months during my crisis.

As Mady works through her big feelings, she insists on being the "little spoon."

"Being the little spoon is the best because it makes you feel safe," she says. I tend to agree.

To ensure she feels safe, I tuck her underneath my arms while she turns her body away from me. It's easier for her to talk to me about her big feelings when we aren't face-to-face. As we settle in, I whisper open-ended questions into her ear to help her sort through what she is feeling and thinking.

In between whispers and muffled cries, we work through the toughest of her worries. After the tears subside, we fall asleep to the audio story of *The Velveteen Rabbit*[2]. A beloved childhood classic, it depicts the story of a little boy and his stuffed bunny, which is quickly discarded in favor of the more elaborate Christmas presents he has received. Thus, the Velveteen Rabbit sits inside a nursery with numerous other toys.

During his time there, he meets the wisest of all the toys, the Skin Horse, who has been in the nursery for decades and had once belonged to the little boy's uncle. One night, the Skin Horse tells the Velveteen Rabbit about the magic of becoming "Real."

"Real isn't how you are made," the Skin Horse says. "It's a thing that happens to you. When a child loves you for a long, long time, not just to play with, but *really* loves you, then you become Real."

"Generally, by the time you are Real, most of your hair has been loved off, and your eyes drop out, and you get loose in your joints and very shabby."

One night, the little boy cannot find the stuffed animal he usually sleeps with, so his grandmother grabs the Velveteen Rabbit from the nursery to comfort him. After that night, the little boy and the rabbit were never far from each other. Exploring the world together brings the Velveteen Rabbit a tremendous amount of joy, which also distracts the rabbit from the noticeable signs of becoming Real.

---

2    Williams, Margery. *The Velveteen Rabbit*. Tullamarine, Australia: Bolinda Publishing Party, Ltd., 2015, audiobook.

"The little rabbit was very happy. So happy that he never noticed how his beautiful velveteen fur was getting shabbier and shabbier, and his tail becoming unsewn, and all the pink rubbed off his nose where the Boy had kissed him."

Whenever that line is read, Mady usually brings Chinny close to her face and kisses his unrecognizable beak. I believe this is her way of letting Chinny know: "This is *our* story."

Chinny the chinstrap penguin became my daughter's best friend when she was two years old. Back then, he was fluffy with a white belly lined in gray fur. He had bright orange claws and black plastic eyes. Stitched onto his side was a tag that read "Chinstrap Penguin." After we had brought the penguin home, I read the tag aloud to Mady and she playfully pointed to him and said, "Chinny."

When I placed Chinny into her arms for the first time, it was kismet. From that point forward, Mady and Chinny were inseparable. Chinny accompanied Mady to daycare, sat with her during family movie nights, and affectionately rode in the cup holder of her brown Graco stroller.

Today, Chinny looks nothing like he did the day Mady first held him in her arms. Chinny has been loved mightily for many years and, much like the Velveteen Rabbit, his age now shows. Not only is the well-loved Chinny missing both eyes, but our dog Lily also likes to retrieve him, take him underneath our bed, and chew on his plastic parts.

My husband has sewn Chinny's claws back together several times using miscellaneous fabric parts to reconstruct the claw's former likeness. Mady calls these reconstruction sessions "surgery" because Chinny's parts get rearranged and switched out. Despite regular surgical procedures, Chinny looks nothing like the bright shiny toy he once was. However, Mady believes Chinny is the most beautiful penguin alive, and no one could ever convince her otherwise.

Sometimes, when Chinny is in public with us, little children will walk by and point at him, making a statement such as "Why doesn't she get a new stuffed animal?" or "That stuffed animal is really old."

Mady is accustomed to these comments. She brushes them off and says to me, "One day, they will love someone as much as I love Chinny. Then they will understand."

She has taken the words from *The Velveteen Rabbit* to heart: "These things don't matter at all, because once you are Real you can't be ugly, except to people who don't understand."

On this particular evening, as Mady and I are listening to the familiar story, the words of *The Velveteen Rabbit* are illuminating things in my heart I have not yet seen. I wipe tears away from my cheeks quietly as not to disrupt Mady's special moment with Chinny. I speak the parts I know by heart through pursed lips as she drifts off to sleep in my arms. Now, more than ever, my soul has a deep recognition that this story belongs to my daughter and me equally.

As the narrator reads each line, I am transported back into my journey of becoming Real.

## I Am Real.

I do not know the exact moment I became Real, but suddenly I am aware I have been loved out of crisis.

As my daughter falls asleep, I revisit the past few months. Like the Velveteen Rabbit, there are a series of small seemingly insignificant moments that have called me into being and out of crisis.

My personal journey to becoming Real began by being broken. I needed the reckoning of crisis to become the truest, real version of myself. Crisis was not gentle, and it destroyed everything I once knew. But crisis was exactly what I needed to experience my breakthrough.

In the middle of my brokenness, my husband asked me that startling question—"What do you want to do with your life?"—which prompted us to find the home that would become the Historic Browning Inn. My brother-in-law Jack painted every inch of The Browning's walls. My friend Maki reminded me of the importance of accepting the truth of my story. My friend Melissa spent countless hours at The Browning decorating, picking out furniture and listening to my heartbreak. And my friend Jodi walked with me for countless hours hearing the truth of my story.

Because of the love of the people around me, I was able to face my pain, accept the truth of my story, begin working with my loved ones through the pain of the affair, and rise from the ashes. The ashes from which I rose were remnants of a past life I hardly recognized as my own. Rising from the ashes of my former life, I located the love I needed for myself inside the actions of others. I had been loved into being. Crisis was the gift I never wanted, but I desperately needed.

My path to becoming Real began with the actions of people loving me through the most difficult period of my life. My husband and family stuck with me as I processed it all. Their big and small actions spoke the most beautiful truths about my life, which sounded like this:

*You are worthy of love and belonging even when you make mistakes.*

*This story does not define you. It is only one chapter.*

*We will love you through crisis and beyond.*

I had been feeling less than human, but like the Velveteen Rabbit and Chinny, I had been loved into being—and into being the real me. From this point forward, I could never be ugly again, except to the people who did not understand.

As the narrator reads the last few lines of *The Velveteen Rabbit*, my mind is drawn back to the present moment. My daughter is fast asleep, tightly holding on to her well-worn and well-loved penguin companion. To people who have not loved this way, Chinny would appear to be an ugly, old object only worthy of discarding. To Mady, Chinny is the most beautiful stuffed animal ever and perfect just as he is. I think he is, too.

As the story ends, I whisper prayers quietly into the universe for my Mady.

*Dear One: May you always remember the beauty and power of well-loved belongings. I pray you maintain a handful of people who you can hold dear and love just like Chinny. I hope when you lose your way, those people will love you through it. I pray you have the courage to do the same for them.*

## From Me to You

You may not be able to see it now, but your difficult story is meant for you.

One day, you will have your Velveteen Rabbit moment. These moments of revelation have a way of visiting us when we least expect them. Chances are you'll be driving to work one idle Tuesday and it will hit you: You don't remember the last time you cried in morning. Or perhaps, you'll be sitting on your deck sipping a hot cup of coffee on a crisp morning in October and it will hit you: The worst part of crisis is finally over. You will come to the realization that you have survived one of your life's most challenging chapters, yet you are still standing.

For a while you may have forgotten what it was like to live, to feel and to breathe. The world continued in the background of your existence while you stayed still. All you could do to get through each day was focus on making the next right decision; some days, you couldn't even do that. But today, you are sipping hot coffee and reminded there is a life to live. For the first time in months, you might even feel like you have the courage to live it.

Crisis has a way of revealing the things that truly matter, the people in whom you should invest, the truths that got you through, the stories that no longer serve you, and the recognition of your strength. These types of personal transformations occur in two parts: before crisis and after crisis. As you end your time through the worst parts of crisis, the person you become will be different than the person you once knew. While remnants of your former life will still exist, you will never be the same.

If you're feeling particularly brave and inspired by change, I'd love to meet you in Part II: Changed.

# Part II:
## *Changed*

*Sometimes life is lived through the colors of fall: rich maroons, bright oranges and vibrant yellows. Fall signals a time for change and a time to release the things in our life that no longer add to its beauty. In this phase, we clear out old patterns, beliefs and ways of doing things that no longer serve us. It allows us to re-evaluate what we want and what we do not. This magical season prepares us to make space to rearrange our lives in a more authentic way.*

# Chapter 8

## What Got You Here, Won't Get You There

---❤---

Sitting down with a newspaper reporter on a brand-new tan sofa with decorative pillows at the Historic Browning Inn, I am wearing grubby cleaning clothes and zero makeup. I cannot remember the last time I showered, and I am embarrassed by my appearance. It is one week before we welcome our first guests.

The previous week, the local reporter currently sitting across from me called wanting an interview about the Historic Browning. During our discussion, he made it clear he wanted to run the story before we open. Because of his insistence and my desire to capitalize on the free marketing opportunity, I reluctantly scheduled our discussion despite my extremely packed pre-opening day schedule.

Because I am constantly running from one thing to the next, I forget to put this important appointment on my calendar after we get off the phone. This mistake landed me in the current situation: sitting on the sofa in my disheveled and unprepared state. I want to apologize for my appearance, but I don't because this confession will reveal I forgot our appointment and might reflect poorly on me.

Instead, I offer the reporter coffee, water, or soda. "I would love a cup of coffee," he exclaims.

I get up from the couch, tug at the bottom of my paint-stained shirt, and head to the kitchen. As I'm preparing his coffee, I run to the nearby laundry room to see if I have any clothes I can change into. I find the back-up blazer I brought from home for unexpected moments like these. I try to put the blazer on over my t-shirt, but no matter how much I fuss with it, it looks ridiculous with my yoga pants and t-shirt. I survey the laundry room looking for additional items to help with my wardrobe malfunction. Nothing.

Recognizing my absence has extended way beyond the normal amount of time it takes to make coffee, I yell from the kitchen,

"Would you like any cream or sugar with your coffee?"

"No. Black is good."

Before I grab his coffee, I quickly glance at my reflection in the microwave glass, fluffing my hair and pulling it behind my ears. As I'm returning from the kitchen, he pulls out his phone and says, "Do you mind if I record this session?"

I've sat through several interviews recently and not one reporter has asked to record our session. I'm not sure why, but I feel uneasy as he places his phone in the middle of the coffee table.

Sensing my nervousness, he says, "It's only so I can listen to it later and make sure I get the quotes right."

"Okay," I respond hesitantly.

I've shared the story hundreds of times in the past four months. Every line has been carefully rehearsed. However, this interview is somehow off-putting, and this reporter is somehow different. It's as if he's searching for something deeper in comparison to the others. He seems to want more than rehearsed lines. I'm afraid he's going to dissect every word. Because of my fear and general disheveled state, my usually passionate, charismatic and well-spoken demeanor seems to be deserting me.

The reporter starts with the standard subset of questions the other reporters have asked of me, which eases my nerves. Right before I'm about to let my guard down, he does what I initially expected and dives into difficult questions.

"You were so unhappy in corporate America; are you happy now owning the Historic Browning?"

I pause for what seems like an eternity and think to myself silently, "What kind of question is that? Am I happy now?"

I dodge his attempts to pry deeper into my current emotional state and stick to the script. I provide the answer to a question he didn't even ask.

"The moment I saw this house I knew it was meant for our family," I say. "It was the next part of our story."

He doesn't take the bait and asks again.

"But really, Liesl . . . are you happy now?"

He calls me by my first name like we know each other. The way he says it assumes we are intimately connected in some way, and I don't like it. His question is invasive, and I don't know him. It makes me angry, but I remain composed. I am the queen of remaining calm. I have control over this narrative. I am happy to put him in his place.

"I'll be happier when we are open. Getting everything ready to open has been totally overwhelming. This is the hard part of entrepreneurship."

He moves on, "You've changed a lot about your life recently, from the corporate life to entrepreneurship, working in human resources to working in hospitality, suit jackets to what you have on now. I think we all want to know, what have you changed about yourself?"

I'm annoyed, "Didn't you just answer your own question? I've changed pretty much everything about myself recently."

"Sure, you picked an entirely new story. That's not what I'm asking. I want to know what's changed about you. How are you different than the person you were living the corporate life?"

I don't have words. I'm not sure what is happening. I have lost control of this conversation.

I am about to cry. I cannot cry in front of this reporter.

"I have to go to the restroom," I blurt out.

I'm visibly shaken as I walk to the bathroom and shut the door. I grab a handful of Kleenex, take several deep breaths, and blot the corners of each eye.

After five minutes, I return composed.

Instead of pushing me further, he sticks to the usual canned questions. Even his hunt for radical candor cannot compete with the emotional state he witnessed in me before I left the room. As we wrap up and he packs away his notepad and tape recorder, I point out the stunning original stained-glass window in the living room, make small talk, and take the empty coffee cup from his hand.

As I shut the door behind him, I murmur under my breath, "Am I happy? What have you changed about yourself?"

Self-righteously, I remind myself that of course I am happy. The Historic Browning is everything I have ever wanted. My marriage and family life are finally on the right track." The mere insinuation that I'm somehow unhappy is insulting to me.

In an effort to brush off the interview, I begin busying myself with opening-day tasks and continue onward. The distraction does not last long. As I cross off items on my to-do list, it becomes harder to ignore the reporter's two probing questions.

That evening, I return home to my family and begin the usual routine of cooking dinner. My husband asks how the interview went. I want to avoid this subject because I'm unsure of how to respond. After replaying the interview in my mind all day, I wonder if there are answers inside those two loaded questions that I need to wrap up. I need time to sit with them before I share my thoughts.

I respond to my husband's inquiry with little enthusiasm, hoping we can move off the topic quickly.

"It was just like all the other interviews," I say.

My lack of excitement regarding the topic surprises Harlen, but he doesn't push further.

"Well, I'm really looking forward to reading it," he says.

To change the subject, I ask questions about his day and continue making tacos.

In the middle of our discussion, an alert pops up on my phone. The reporter has sent a recording of our interview via e-mail. Seeing his name in my inbox makes me queasy. As if dodging the reporter's question wasn't arduous enough, my uneasiness is now recorded for me to relive.

After working through four months of crisis, this is the first signal that something isn't right. Likely, there had been other signs, but perhaps subconsciously, I was staying busy so I wouldn't have to read these signs. Up until this point, I believed everything about my newfound direction was exactly where I need to be heading.

While simmering taco meat on the stove, I begin to wonder if listening to the interview might be helpful in untangling those two loaded questions: Am I happy? What have your changed about yourself?"

I'm fearful of listening to the recording, but aware that doing so might help uncover a truth I need to hear. I stay quiet most of dinner and try to pay attention to the collective stories each member of my family is relating around the table. As much as I try to be present, my mind is hyper-fixated on that unsettling interview.

After clearing dishes and running the bedtime routine, I decide I must face my fear and listen to the recording. I kiss everyone goodnight, then retreat to my bedroom. Usually, Harlen watches TV for at least an hour before he comes upstairs. I self-righteously think to myself, "Well, that's another thing that has changed. My husband and I sleep in the same room again." I begin fishing in my nightstand drawer for my Bluetooth earbuds to listen to the recording before he comes up—and before I lose my courage.

I sit in bed, pull up the recording on my phone, and reluctantly hit play. I listen intently to each line.

All my answers leading up to those two dreaded questions mirror the standard responses I gave to previous reporters. The tone of the interview changes when I reach the part where he asks, "Are you happy?" I sound nervous, my voice cracks and I pause a lot.

These questions are meant for me, but I am petrified of the true answers.

I start playing the recording again. My canned lines are polished, uplifting and romantic. They sound like the plot of a Hallmark holiday movie: "Former corporate HR strategist leaves the sixty-plus-hour grind to open a charming inn in a suburb of Kansas City. On her journey, she finds the meaning in her life for which she's always been looking."

This bright, shiny story is the perfect soundbite for casual grocery store run-ins with acquaintances, interviews with reporters, and the "About Us" section on the Historic Browning website. It is a splendid story.

Hearing my own voice reciting this story to yet another person, I face the realization that my internal change is incredibly small in comparison to the dramatic shift in my narrative. I have accepted the truth of my story and begun the healing process. However, I ask myself the question: Had I needed this dramatic polished story to save me because I had not known how to save myself? Did I need this narrative to serve as a mirage while I was putting back together all the broken pieces?

I come to the realization that if I don't continue doing the internal work necessary to change the patterns and routines that landed me inside crisis, this new and beautiful story will end up being as much of a nightmare as the last one.

This story was not my salvation. No matter how right it was for our family, this story cannot do the work for me.

For a while, the Hallmark holiday movie soundbite served as

the protection I needed to avoid exposing my truth. While I was working through the hardest parts of crisis, I needed this romantic story for a grand form of misdirection. I couldn't handle the vulnerability wrapped up in one more person asking me, "Are you doing okay?" I felt weak admitting aloud I wasn't doing okay. Instead, I lied by sharing an over-the-top story that my former perfectionist achiever self-crafted.

A week before we opened the Historic Browning Inn, the annoying reporter (who is now an exceptionally good friend) asked me two life-changing questions that forced me to look inside myself. He made me realize true transformation was not a matter of simply aligning my life to the right story; it was about embracing my internal changes and being honest with people so I could become the next version of who I was meant to be.

On another note, the reporter-turned-friend would tell you the first time we met he was certain he had made a new friend. His perspective of this story is so far off from mine, I am even more cognizant now of just how buried I was. He still asks me the hard questions and it is my favorite thing about him.

## From Me to You

When we make major life decisions, we expect these decisions to save us. We believe a new city, a new marriage or a new career will be the change we need to move forward with our lives. We are unaware that choosing this new story is, at its core, running away from the old one. Inside our newfound path, we often continue living out the same patterns and routines that landed us in crisis in the old story.

The newness of a fresh story temporarily tricks us into believing we have truly changed. We get caught up in the romance of a new relationship, career, city, church or friendship. This honeymoon phase fuels the temporary belief that we also have changed internally. We don't recognize the honeymoon phase of experiencing something new is the easy part.

Like all starry-eyed firsts, the newness eventually wears off. You realize the numerous yoga classes in Bali that once inspired you during your travels are as dull as the Seattle coffeeshop scene you left behind. In your current state, this dullness can come from your inability to appreciate the beauty in all places.

Eventually, the elation from the fancy holiday proposal and your subsequent honeymoon in Cozumel transition into your first fight, during which you still have no idea how to communicate your feelings. The result: another divorce, another job quit, another new city.

I love this quote from Marshall Goldsmith, an executive leadership coach and educator: "What got you here, won't get you there."

This is an important truth: You cannot simply choose a new or better story and expect it to save you. It doesn't matter how right the story is for you. To save yourself, you must do the internal work to discover why you keep repeating old, harmful patterns. You must change your behaviors and habits to get a different, positive result.

For example, you might need to address your propensity to avoid conflict, which can result in never having a healthy relationship, no matter how right the person is for you. Or perhaps, you don't recognize that your inability to say "No" at work will lead to burnout, no matter how perfect the job. Circumstances cannot change you; only you have the power to change your circumstances.

Living through brokenness is only the first step. Unless you are willing to take a hard look at the patterns that landed you inside crisis, you will end up right back where you started. To arrange your new life in accordance with your old self will not get you to the next place that is meant for you.

## As you transition into the newness of change, here are some things I learned that I hope will help you:

* **Lean into the "suckiness" of change.**

  My editor informed me *suckiness* is not an actual word. However, it is the only word to adequately describe the challenges I encountered in this change phase. When you are shifting, there are some parts your "old self" and some parts your "new self." The transition between the "now" version of you to the "next" version of you is clunky. Figuring out which parts of your old existence still fit into your new reality can be jarring. Because I'm your honest friend, I'm not going to sugar-coat this part for you. It sucks. Your old life and your new life will be at odds with each other. They will fight for your attention and you will feel like you are living inside two worlds. Not all shifts will be this dramatic in your life. When you find yourself smack down in the middle of crisis, however, the shifts necessary to prioritize your higher good will be extreme.

Because of the significant crisis you have been through, your core values and lifestyle likely will be dramatically altered. Crisis is an earth-shattering experience for most of us and expecting to make it to the other side unchanged is not realistic. This doesn't mean the life you lived before was necessarily inauthentic or should be discarded completely. However, accept there are parts that felt authentic to you before that no longer fit now. Some parts of your former life will impede your progress if you don't eliminate them. While you are not scrapping your entire existence, you are deciding which parts will fit in your new reality.

I didn't realize how desperately my old life wanted me back until I started pursuing my new one. Once I moved passed the worst parts of crisis, several of my good-time friends came out the woodwork. They wanted to have driveway drinks again, see the inn and pick up where we left off. They wanted to ignore their grand exit from my life and enjoy my company as I began my climb toward new heights. I imagine many of them didn't know what to say when I hit my bottom. I have no ill will toward any of my old good-time friends. As much as I sometimes wanted to go back, I couldn't. It doesn't mean I didn't try.

Because your old life will fight to have you back, there will be comfort in returning to your old patterns, beliefs and routines. These old ways are familiar and easy to you. While you know they are about as good for you as eating an entire pint of chunky monkey ice cream in one sitting, the result is at least predictable. Your brain is hardwired for predictability and it will choose certainty over discomfort every time. While there is temporary comfort hidden in your old life, it eventually will disappoint you. Honor and recognize that disappointment for what it is.

Moving outside of crisis requires you to lean into the suckiness of change. Leaning in requires the acceptance of this truth: You are dramatically shifting planes of existence. While you are shifting, your old plane and your new plane will fight for first place. Remember, not all changes in your life will be this dramatic. This shift is particularly jarring only because you are completely rebuilding.

- **Focus on what you have gained.**

After crisis, it is easy to focus on what you have lost. Most likely, you've lost a great deal on this journey. You've lost beliefs about yourself that felt certain a short time ago. It's possible you've lost friends who fell off the radar during your difficult time. You've let go of old patterns that no longer serve you. People rarely talk about the losses that accompany change. If you are approaching change correctly, there will be mourning and loss. There is no other way.

Spoken from experience, ruminating on your losses will not help you move forward. Instead, focus on the space those losses have created for you to form the next person you are meant to become. While that space might feel expansive right now, it is meant to be filled. You will be tempted to fill it with the remnants from your old life, and at times you will. That's okay. You will need these reminders to clarify why these things no longer fit or make you feel alive.

When you are ready, start exploring the possibilities that exist inside the wide-open space. Focus on reinventing yourself day by day. Perhaps you've always wanted to have coffee with that awkward mom in your neighborhood who wears the "I'm not for everyone" t-shirt. Or maybe you've always wanted to start a side hustle as a virtual assistant outside of your regular job.

My husband and I filled our wide-open spaces with so many new things. We started intentional weekly walks focused on bettering our relationship. We spent summer evenings at the pool with our children. I focused on growing the business at the Historic Browning Inn. We invested our time and energy into our crisis-proof friends.

Fill those spaces with better habits, soothing routines and people who encourage you to choose your best life.

- **Take a stand for your new life.**

To continue your evolution post-crisis, you need to start making hard choices. You will have to take a stand for your new life. As a wise person once said, "If you stand for nothing, you'll fall for anything." Taking a stand involves making hard choices that can be incredibly uncomfortable.

As you become more aware of the things that no longer fit with your latest evolution, it will be important to rearrange your life accordingly. This can be the most difficult part of the journey. There will be friends, family, organizations, potentially your job and people to whom you have committed your time that no longer fit this new iteration.

My husband I spent hours one-on-one and in therapy evaluating the changes we needed to make that would allow us to heal and move forward with our lives. Some of these changes were easy; others were not. Shortly after the affair, we both decided increasing our communication was of the utmost importance. This change was not hard for us. We texted each other more, discussed our feelings regularly and carved out time for long walks.

Other changes were much harder. During one of our talks, Harlen pointed out a close friendship he believed was impeding our progress. This friendship was established while I was on a destructive path. I had matched energies with this person and attracted her in my life because we were on remarkably similar journeys. I enabled her bad decisions and she encouraged mine. Harlen pointed this out and made it clear this friendship was not healthy for us. He believed my insides were finally beginning to match my outsides, minus this one relationship. He challenged me to either get this friend on board with our new direction or politely move on.

At first, his observation upset me, and I thought he was callous for even suggesting I cut ties with this friend. I believed she and I had been through a difficult time together and she had been there for me. My husband reminded me she was there for me by encouraging the affair and engaging in similar destructive behaviors. This was the role we both played in each other's lives. I take accountability for playing an equally toxic role in her life.

It was not easy, but part of embracing the suckiness of change was moving forward without that friendship. It was not personal, yet it was deeply personal. It hurt me tremendously to lose this person from my life. I desperately wanted her to be honest with herself about our combined web of lies. Unfortunately, she was not ready to take the leap with me. There were many times I wasn't ready to take that journey with others either. I wish only the best for her life and recognize we are all on our own journey. While our paths were no longer compatible, I'm certain she felt the same way about me.

- **Accept that change will happen in waves**

The process of change is equal parts painful and beautiful. Unfortunately, any good transformation takes time. There are no short-cuts to doing the hard work. If someone tells you otherwise, they are selling you something. While we all want to wake up one morning and be a new person, it never happens that way. Arriving at a full-blown crisis took years of bad choices; they can't be undone overnight. Give yourself time and have grace when you make mistakes.

Leaning into change required both Harlen and I to prioritize our higher good. It was necessary for both of us to make a series of hard choices. During our healing, we kept many things the same, but so much also changed. We rebuilt the foundation of our lives together slowly and learned not to apologize for it. There were things to which we had both committed our time that were no longer inspiring in our new lives. As we shifted, we both changed careers, some friendships and our priorities. Building our new foundation took four years. I repeat: It took four years.

It would have saved us both a great deal of time if all the choices we needed to make presented themselves simultaneously. Instead, these choices came in waves. Thankfully, these waves kept us from becoming completely overwhelmed by the need to immediately change everything. They emerged one by one. As you are standing inside a wave of change, listen deeply to your inner voice. This voice will guide you. When you really tune in, it will become abundantly clear the things that no longer belong in your life.

Once your inner voice illuminates the things that need changed, don't fight it. Often, we fight change in our lives because we believe we must remain loyal to people, organizations, jobs, neighbors and rituals instead of honoring the truth inside ourselves. You are not required to sacrifice the person you have become for anyone else's comfort. Crisis has shown you new truths, revealed your true friends and clarified your purpose. It is time to let go of anything that no longer serves the person you have become.

You do not need to apologize for this. I repeat: You do not need to apologize for this. Living this difficult story has changed you. To arrange your life in accordance with your old self will not get you to the next place that is meant for you. Lean into the changes and embrace the new choices you need to make.

# Chapter 9

## *Discounts*

---❤️---

Opening day finally arrived at the Historic Browning Inn and our entire family was elated.

Dewy-eyed and naïve, I was confident the toughest part of our story was behind us. Afterall, in the past four months, I had survived the worst of crisis and moved on to the next chapter of our family's story. The broken woman who turned in her company badge, computer and the corporate hustle had begun transforming her life. Certainly, the road forward would be paved with success and ease.

With many achievements accomplished in a few short months, a false sense of confidence permeated the Historic Browning's opening. The day began with last-minute preparations for the arrival of our first guests. While scrubbing the knotty pine floors in the kitchen on my hands and knees, I blasted holiday music through my phone.

On social media, I posted, "Find a job where you can wear yoga pants, blare holiday music and call it work. #entrepreneurlife" As a flood of comments poured in praising my latest accomplishments, I made a mental checklist of everything we had done to properly prepare to open our small business.

We had carefully considered the competitive landscape around us. Downtown Lee's Summit, Missouri, desperately needed an alternative hospitality option, and the Historic Browning would be a niche player. At the time, no other local inns existed anywhere near The Browning. The competing local hotel chains were not in walkable distance of the popular downtown district and they catered to a completely different market than we did. Check.

We had thoroughly curated local support and buy-in from the community. Being the new kid on the block had its perks. The community embraced me with coffee invitations, business membership opportunities and a seat at the table. The Historic Browning and I were featured in several local media publications. Check.

Our meticulous business plan and its many pages covered all the bases. Sure, we had taken out a hefty loan with a high interest rate to cover our startup expenses and the property, but we would begin generating revenue soon. If our revenue mirrored those projected in our business plan, we would certainly make it. Plus, I believed our revenue targets were conservative. Meeting our three-month, six-month and twelve-month goals looked promising. Check.

As I checked in our first guests on that cold November day, I was beaming with absolute pride. Handing over the keys, I saw the guest's absolute delight as she eyed the property. Our family had built something truly beautiful.

Creating the Historic Browning together had pushed us out of the most difficult part of our story. While driving home from the inn after its opening day, I had an absolute sense of happiness. In hindsight, it was probably an ordinary sense of happiness, but happiness had become a foreign emotion to me when I was working sixty hours a week and living out my unhappiness through an affair.

As I drove further and further away from an old story that no longer served me, I was blissfully unaware of the difficult journey ahead. Rebuilding my life after crisis would not be the small four-month project I had assumed. I had taken on the demanding challenge of entrepreneurship, which is a large enough task without the fresh sting of crisis added into the mix. While I don't want to discount the high that I felt that day or diminish the accomplishments, it would be insincere to say I was a totally new woman.

While the worst was over, the universe knew I needed the discomfort of change to push me beyond the patterns that landed me in the thick of crisis in the first place. Entrepreneurship would be one of the many teachers I needed to force me outside my comfort zone. Although I was afforded a much-needed momentary high on the inn's opening day, the most difficult part of change was ready to push me rather abruptly into the next version of who I was meant to be. The lessons wrapped inside entrepreneurship began immediately—whether I was ready or not.

In the first three months, we operated on a shoestring budget because our working capital went below $10,000 in the bank account. Yet, I held tightly to the belief that if I built something fantastically impressive, people would come. This assumption was the fuel that kept me moving at an energizer bunny pace.

When we launched our online reservation site, my delusions began to dissolve. The preparations to launch the site took weeks of planning and implementation. For the first three months of operation, I had created daily goals as to the number of reservations we would receive. I estimated we would book twenty reservations the day we launched.

The excitement I felt the day the reservation site went live invigorated me. I worked with Harlen on managing the kids that morning in preparation for the big launch. I got up at 5:00 a.m. and posted on all our social media channels. Then, I sat back and waited for the projected reservations to roll in. I began checking my phone and email every five minutes for the anticipated flood of new clients that likely would surpass my original estimation.

Spoiler alert: It didn't happen.

At the end of the day, we had two reservations; both were good friends. Convinced the first day was hardly representative of our future success, I furiously began emailing everyone I knew. Most evenings, I reached out to anyone remotely connected to our area. I knew if even half of the enthusiastic supporters we have garnered would make one reservation, we would more than meet our projected targets.

By the end of the week, even after all my attempts, we had only one additional reservation. By the end of the month, we had a grand total of four. What kept me up late at night was wondering where everyone had disappeared after attending our expensive ribbon cutting.

This lackluster start continued months after opening. We failed to hit the three-month, six-month and twelve-month targets outlined in our business plan.

Looking back, I now recognize I was overly confident in my acumen and brilliant business decisions, a trait many novice entrepreneurs share. My delusions of grandeur were so inflated as I drove away on opening day, I ignored how under-capitalized and wholly unprepared I was for this venture in an unfamiliar industry.

Many entrepreneurs go through this phase. With a zeal equivalent to honeymoon-like euphoria, we are certain and excited about our new business. Like a new marriage, everyone rallied around us with enthusiasm: a ribbon-cutting celebration, media coverage, constant social media showering and well-wishes. This phase reinforces the belief that success is imminent.

But after the newness wears off, reality settles in and things get real. The bills begin to appear, but the revenue does not. When we don't hit our projected business plan targets, we are in full-on panic mode. We realize acquiring customers is going to take much more hustling than we thought. Many of us are under-capitalized, locked into SBA loans with high interest rates, and struggling to make ends meet.

The first year owning the Historic Browning was deflating, which caused me to fall back into several of my old patterns. I began frantically working sixty hours a week again and saying *yes* to everyone. I was exhausted.

To acquire customers, I began giving massive discounts whenever someone asked. My inability to say "No," which was the driving force behind my corporate burnout, now was part of my latest story. These discounts were significantly below my asking price. As I scraped by to pay the bills for this mess I created, I convinced myself I was "lucky" to get any type of new business. In moments of clarity, I would flash back to my corporate days and remember feeling "lucky" to be asked to fulfill all the last-minute requests. I remember thinking, "I know I'm up at 1:00 a.m., but I should be grateful. I live a life most people dream of. I'm asked to do all these high-priority projects. Most people never have a life like mine."

As the business continued to lose money, it was draining our personal finances. The burden it placed on our family weighed heavily on me every day. We had already been through so much, and now my what-would-you-do-if-you-could-do-anything venture was threatening our livelihood.

My decision to move forward with this dream was causing deep shame for me. The guilt ate at my insides as each of our personal credit card balances grew closer and closer to maxing out. Furthermore, I felt singularly responsible for putting us in this hole. Leaving my safe corporate job for a dream now felt foolish. One of my worst fears was confirmed: Imagining and wanting big dreams are not for responsible women with families.

I began listening to the voices around me instead of the one inside of me. Listening to the outside voices meant hustling to meet the demands of everyone but myself. This trajectory was an old familiar pattern: hustle for your worthiness, please everyone outside yourself, then burn out.

The opposing voice inside of me who had urged me to pursue this dream remained calm, still and certain. She spoke to me during the worst part of crisis. Her presence was recognizable when I had hit the bottom and was crying on the dirty floor inside a sea of cubicles. I could still hear her, "It's time for you to leave. It's past time for you to go. There is nothing left for you here. Pick up that box containing the remnants of your career and walk out those doors."

Her strong voice had guided me to this new story, and she knew the way out of this mess. She was ready to help me move forward with the changes I needed to make to stay on my path. The stress of entrepreneurship, however, had propelled me back into old patterns because they were familiar. The result: a shame spiral that felt almost as miserable as the last day at my corporate job.

This shame eventually transitioned into full-blown resentment. My primary target of this resentment were people who asked for discounts for the pleasure of staying at my inn. They would drive up in Acuras, trash my bridal suite, and smear dark chocolate all over my bright white comforters. I silently cussed them out as I cleaned their rooms with our onsite manager. I felt held captive to their ridiculous requests and powerless not to comply. I needed their money to stay afloat. I didn't believe I could turn down any revenue, no matter how deep the discounts, how outlandish the demands or how much the disregard of decorum.

In my mind, these discount pushers were rude, entitled and totally unaware of what it took to run a small business. I assumed they were trying to make me mad on purpose.

Whenever I was cooking breakfast for guests, I was regularly asked, "Did you inherit this property from your parents?"

"I wish," I would think, barely resisting saying: "Now that you know I have a massive mortgage, would you be so kind as to pay me full price for your stay, you cheapskate?"

To any of my family and friends who would listen, I regularly complained about these discount pushers. In moments of clarity, this complaining was familiar to me. During these resentment sessions about the inn, I often was met with this constructive feedback: "Liesl, you need to establish healthy boundaries with people. Just tell them 'No.' This is your business, and you have the right to ask for full price so you can pay your bills and feed your family."

Saying *no* was a novel idea to me. It definitely was not something I had done in the corporate world. Whenever someone brought up this idea of boundaries to me, I'd get excited about even the thought of telling someone *no*. The call for change was so strong.

Unfortunately, I soon realized it was easy to do in theory, but much harder do to in practice. Recognizing my need for boundaries was the first step, but the skill of setting boundaries was far more challenging. A discount pusher would call, and I still couldn't face the idea of turning down desperately needed revenue. I would cave. Regularly entertaining and ultimately accepting requests for discounts meant our business was doing more work for less money. I was perpetually cranky, relentlessly hustling and utterly exhausted.

Then, one Sunday, as I was angrily scrubbing the guest bathtub and marinating in my own misery, the silence invited the calm, reassuring and certain voice. She always showed up so clearly in the quiet moments.

*Have you considered that you have more power in this situation than you realize? You own this business. You're not working for someone else now. Hence, you have complete con-*

*trol over your pricing. You know exactly how much money you need to make on each room to pay the bills. So why is it someone else's fault when you accept payment below the value of what you need?*

*Most of these so-called discount pushers are not trying to offend you. They ask many businesses they patronize for discounts. They are negotiating.*

*If a business owner tells a client there is no discount, the client either pays full price or takes their business elsewhere. If these people choose to take their business elsewhere, let them because you cannot afford to host them. They are not your people.*

*You are the one responsible for allowing this treatment. You always have been. This is a pattern in your life that led you to your last crisis. You have not identified standards for your business, yourself or your family. Without identifying your own standards, you cannot create boundaries.*

## As I let the wise words of my inner voice sink in, I began to inventory a list of life examples of my inability to say *no* and to ask for what I needed.

### Example 1:

I am sitting with my boss in her office. We have a huge presentation scheduled for early the next morning. I have done all the legwork and spent hours preparing this presentation. As we are reviewing the PowerPoint, my boss gets hyper-fixated on Slide 4. It's a bubble chart. She asks me if the data is proportionate to the size of the bubbles. I tell her it's close. She wants it to be precisely accurate.

Instead of telling her I have no idea how to figure this out, I immediately say, "Yes, I can do that." I don't ask for help. I don't ask for clarification as to why this is so important. Instead, I work past midnight trying to figure it out while crying. After hours of work, I surrender and ask my husband, the data scientist, to run it through a statistical program. He sends me the result. The bubbles are off by less than a centimeter.

I am resentful and angry that this had to be changed in the first place. I feel as though my boss doesn't value my time or understand how much work it takes to make her happy. I never bring it up again, but it becomes part of a growing list of complaints I have against her. This list could've been avoided if I would've approached these topics with her.

## Example 2:

I am in college. A woman at the church I attend asks if I will babysit her special-needs son because he connects with me. I love babysitting, need the money and her son is a sweetheart. During our first babysitting experience, I watch her son for more than three hours. When she returns, she puts two dollars down on the table and says, "I know you're not watching him for money. It's so Christ-like to help me out."

I don't know what to say. I need money, yet I feel obligated to help her out because she pointedly reminded me that it is Christ-like. I feel manipulated and powerless to tell her what I need. Instead, I say, "I'm happy to watch him anytime to help you out." I'm embarrassed to tell her I need money to pay my bills. I remind myself her situation is harder than mine and I should help because it is a selfless thing to do.

After months of free babysitting, I grow increasingly bitter and resentful toward her. Instead of talking to her, I stop answering her phone calls all together and avoid her at church.

### Example 3:

During the holidays, we travel to visit my husband's family multiple states away from where we live. My mother-in-law persistently pushes for us to stay at her home. She rarely gets to see us and wants as much time with us as possible.

Traveling with two small children, especially during the holidays, is exceedingly stressful. So, I book a hotel room to give us a place to unwind after each long day of family festivities. My husband's niece lets us know the family is not happy about this lodging arrangement. I lash out at my husband in the hotel room that night because his family is making unreasonable demands. I am once again resentful and angry that no one understands my need for personal space in the evening so I can be the best version of myself during the days we spend with them.

## As I survey these life events, my inner voice leads me to the following realizations:

- **I feel I am held captive to other people's opinions of me.** Their thoughts, feelings and beliefs about me are the foundation of my self-esteem. Because I have not established healthy beliefs about what I value, my worth rests inside what others think of me.
- **I hustle for my own worthiness by being whatever anyone needs me to be.** Because my self-esteem is wrapped up inside the opinions of others, I am constantly

hustling for my worthiness. I become whatever people need and sacrifice my own happiness in the process.

- **The hustle exhausts me, and I feel powerless, angry and resentful**. I wonder how anyone could ask these things of me. I would never ask these things of them. I eventually burn out.

After these revelations, I take a moment to look around the Historic Browning Inn at what my family had created.

Hanging on the walls are pictures my husband hung at 2:00 a.m. the week before we opened. My brother-in-law Jack painted these walls. He had sworn to and had succeeded at covering every room in less than three days. My friend Melissa decorated every inch of the house-turned-guest inn on a shoestring budget, and it was stunning. My daughter, Mady, and my son, Ethan, cleaned every one of the many windows with Windex, buckets of water and sponges the weekend before we opened. Our crisis-proof friends painted trim, labored doing yard work and deep cleaned the entire house.

The Browning was a huge labor of love that not only saved me, but also saved my family. Most notably, we had survived the worst part of crisis. This place was nothing short of magical, and we deserved full price for our efforts.

I realized the call for change in my life was stronger than it had ever been. I could take my old patterns directly into my new story or I could listen to the inner voice who wanted to guide me along in the right direction. I made a choice that day while scrubbing the guest bathtub and listening to my inner voice. Instead of choosing my default operating mode that had landed me in the middle of crisis, I took one bold step in the right direction.

This new direction required that I see the value in what our family and friends had built together. It required me to take a hard look inside myself and at those around me. I had a business. I had a group of irreplaceable, crisis-proof friends. I had a family who had loved me through the worst part of my life.

I was broken, but now I was beginning to change.

It was time for me to ask for what I deserved. While I still had several old patterns to let go of along the way, I never again would entertain another discount pusher.

## From Me to You

This is a topic for which I feel deeply passionate. I believe most of us struggle with boundaries because it is an oversimplified concept.

Self-help mantras emphasize the importance of saying no. They even help us practice different ways of communicating *no* in perfectly crafted phrases. Trust me, I used to have countless pieces of notebook paper filled with *no* prose.

I always knew the moments I should say no. Those moments were not hard for me to identify. I recognized these moments because my stomach would fill with butterflies, my palms would get sweaty and I would feel queasy.

Instead of overcoming my fear and pulling out my *no* prose, I would choose comfort rather than courage. I would slip into my default mode, which was an endless supply of "Yesses," and accommodate everyone at my own expense. Then, I'd resent the person who obviously inflicted their unrealistic demands on me—demands I never would personally ask of anyone.

Every time that I would say *yes* when I wanted to say *no*, I'd feel defeated. But I didn't know how to change my response. The reason many of us struggle with the real practice of setting boundaries is because we have not defined our standards.

## For me, establishing healthy boundaries started with three actions:

1. Determining how I want to feel and who I want to be.
2. Defining standards and criteria regarding how I deserve to be treated.
3. Communicating what I expect from others to protect my standards and my feelings.

Let's build out this example using the discount pushers.

**1. Determining how I want to feel and who I want to be.**
Developing my business standards started by focusing on how I deserved to feel when operating my business. It helped me begin focusing on the guests who brought me joy.

The guests who brought me joy paid full price for my services without complaint. They raved about the breakfast experience, the locally sourced amenities, the stunning seasonal décor, and the proximity to the charming downtown district. They provided thoughtful and reasonable feedback on improving the guest experience. Sometimes, they got chocolate all over the comforters or left the bridal suite a mess, but I didn't resent them because that was part of the price they paid for my services. This helped me put words to "how I want to feel and who I want to be."

**Here it is:** When I am interacting with my clients at the Historic Browning, I want to feel fulfilled, grateful, happy, energized, purpose-filled, ready to serve and a desire to give more. I want to be a joyful inn owner who provides her customers with a top-notch customer service experience.

## 2. Defining standards and criteria regarding how I deserve to be treated.

After defining how I wanted to feel and who I wanted to be, I worked backward. I asked myself, "What helped me achieve this positive state of being?"

Was I resentful about chocolate on pillowcases or the bridal suite in disarray? If so, was I resentful because I wasn't getting the value I needed from these transactions (the value being to pay my bills, support my family and such)? The answer was simple: I was not getting the value I needed from these transactions, which led to resentment. Thus, I set a standard to protect how I wanted to be treated.

**Here it is:** I deserve for my customers to pay full price. Until I had set these standards, I couldn't reasonably enforce a boundary and tell discount-seeking clients they were violating those standards. The result of not having standards was an epic failure.

## 3. Communicating what I expect from others to protect my standards and my feelings.

Saying *no* became much easier when I defined how I wanted to feel and had aligned standards.

**Here it is:** When people ask me for discounts, I politely tell them "No."

While these three steps certainly won't change your life completely, I guarantee if you start practicing them in small areas, you'll be less inclined to freely discount your value.

A quick reminder before we move on: Defining standards for your business and your life does not make you selfish, rude or uncharitable. If you do not spend time articulating how you want to feel and what you deserve, not understanding your value will inevitably follow.

Defining your standards is not always easy. It requires deep reflection about what is and what is not okay for you. Until this happens, you will continue to give too much of yourself and resent those who want you to lower your standards and your value.

## Chapter 10
## Toxic Truths

*D*esperately craving time for myself amid my packed schedule at the Historic Browning, I got up at 5:00 a.m. on a Monday morning and began lacing up my tennis shoes in the dark to take a long walk. After the dreadful Sunday I had the day before, I needed time alone to clear my head.

Nine months prior, we had opened the Historic Browning, and now I had just perpetrated my first enormously sloppy business error. A bride called me frantic on Sunday morning wondering why staff wasn't present to let her party into The Browning. I had completely forgotten about the bridal party we were hosting at the inn. The call came in while I was in my pajamas, coffee in hand and getting ready to enjoy the only day I thought I had off for the entire week.

In the chaos known as my life, I completely forgot to put her reservation in the system. I was frantic, embarrassed and overly apologetic when she called. This was not how I wanted to run my business and it was not reflective of the stellar customer-service experience we usually provided.

To add to this tragic moment, the main floor of the inn hadn't been cleaned since the last party had left. As I feverishly threw on clothes to head to The Browning, I imagined the bride walking into a completely dirty house on one of the most important days of her life. If I were in her shoes, I would most certainly be upset.

Harlen takes one look at me as I am exiting the door and says, "This pattern of over-commitment and working sixty hours a week isn't working for us. After I'm done helping you with this mistake, we need to talk. Now, what can I do to help?"

I ask Harlen to buy a bottle of champagne and flowers as a gift to the bride and meet me at The Browning.

Fortunately, after I arrive at the inn, I was pleasantly surprised the guests who stayed the night before left the home in immaculate condition. They made the beds, cleaned the kitchen, and even left the main floor in incredible shape. As I walked into the main foyer, I was overcome with relief. The good deeds of these Airbnb guests had saved me from total embarrassment and from ruining this bride's wedding day.

Overall, the tragic moment could have been much worse, yet it was still a warning sign from the universe. If a mistake like this happened again, a complimentary bottle of champagne, a percentage of the bridal package refunded and an apologetic inn owner might not be enough to smooth things over.

Lacing up my tennis shoes, I mentally replayed yesterday's events and they continued to loop in my mind as I stepped outside to an unseasonably chilly July morning. I headed back inside my home to grab a hoody for the walk.

Our main floor closet had become a mess of jackets strewn about the floor with little organization. I hated the disarray, but with my demanding schedule I had little time to devote to the state of my own house. I fished through the unruly piles, hoping to find something to keep me warm. After locating my fifteen-year-old Kansas State University hoody, I zipped up my jacket and pull the hood over my head.

The morning was still and quiet. During the busyness of high season at the inn, which generally runs from May to October, I rarely have time for the luxury of stillness. For me, 5:00 a.m. is the only time of day when people don't need anything from me. At this un-godly hour, there is space for me to hear my own thoughts. Plus, I needed time to reflect in preparation for my talk with Harlen. I still hear his words from yesterday, "This isn't working for us."

Walking out the door, I took a deep breath, put in my earbuds and turned on my playlist. Less than a minute into my walk, my busy to-do list decided to occupy more than its fair share of space in my head. The mere thought of everything I must accomplish in the week ahead seemed unmanageable and defeating. In less than two hours, my alert-heavy phone would be blowing up as usual.

The events from the day before and the realization that there are simply not enough hours in the day had overtaken the vigor I typically carry into the morning hours. To attempt to gain some control, I began creating a schedule in my head, outlining how I would spend each hour of the day.

As I was mentally planning out every minute of the day, there was tension in my neck and shoulders, then my chest began to tighten. I became aware there was absolutely no way to accomplish everything this Monday required of me. Nothing seemed optional; everything felt immediate. My decision to take a walk appeared frivolous. I should be using this time more efficiently. I should be knocking out real work so I could start the day a little less buried.

This is a cycle that once again is governing my life. Every day, I do my best to unbury myself of the day's obligations. I answer e-mails from brides asking a thousand different questions; make breakfast for guests; get the kids to school; attend event planning meetings; clean the inn; setup for new guests; attend evening networking events; and then return home half-alive.

As I was considering turning around to do actual work, the Imagine Dragons' song "Whatever It Takes" came on and I was inspired to keep walking. I started singing the lyrics out loud as I rounded the corner of our neighborhood walking trail.

The faster tempo of the song is motivating, and I am moved to transition from a fast walk to a jog. This momentary inspiration lasts for two short blocks before I'm breathy, my left leg hurts and I'm compelled to stop. I've never been much of a runner. All aspirations to fulfill my misplaced dream of running a marathon were literally shattered in April 2016, after I fractured my tibia spring skiing in Vail, Colorado.

No matter how fast the tempo of a song, even the shortest distance spent jogging is a painful reminder of the injury. Yet, here I was doing the thing I knew I should not be doing. As the song ended, I put my hands behind my head to catch my breath and return to walking.

The song had triggered a déjà vu moment. I have been here before. The cadence of my newfound entrepreneurial life feels familiar. Getting up at 5:00 a.m., trying to remember when I last washed my hair and constantly letting everyone down are not new experiences to me.

In that moment, I realized the hustle of the sixty-hour corporate grind I thought I had escaped had traveled with me to my new life.

My whatever-it-takes attitude was the ticket to quickly climb the corporate ladder. It afforded me fast promotions, glamourous moments on a jet and cotton candy martini drinks in a professional sports venue suite. The endpoint to this destination was the loneliest place of my entire existence.

I used to do whatever it took to get ahead at work. This included always being available when someone needed me, responding to e-mails immediately, working during vacations, being the last mom to pick my kids up at daycare and basically doing whatever anyone needed me to do.

For me, doing whatever it took deprived me of my mental health, my family, my vacations and my being present. I could not continue to repeat this pattern. My need to be the martyr for my own success was going to land me right back in crisis. Old Liesl would have found the right dry shampoo to maximize her time and skip showers. New Liesl had to do something different. I had to save myself.

It was time for another rewrite. It was time for a changed perspective: I turned "Whatever it takes" into "Whatever it takes leads to burnout."

"Whatever it takes" is a mantra glorifying hustle, busyness and the belief that success is found in self-sacrifice. While I believe in the value of hard work, there is a subtle, yet danger-ous, line that can be crossed, leading to self-sacrifice.

What does self-sacrifice look like?

For me, self-sacrifice was continuously deprioritizing the things that mattered in my life. Self-sacrifice was forgetting to eat breakfast and lunch because I was so consumed with my work and to-do list. It was getting less than four hours of sleep so I could work on urgent last-minute projects requiring my "imme-diate attention." It was being the last person to pick up my kids at daycare because every e-mail that hit my inbox "deserved" an immediate response. It was a thousand "Yesses" wrapped up inside the belief that success is only possible through sacrifice. No pain, no gain.

Eventually, self-sacrifice becomes a god you can't stop feed-ing. It robs you of a life well lived with the promise of tomor-row's success and the belief that, "One day, I'll have all the money I need to relax. Until then, I'm going to keep hustling."

My previous corporate life wasn't 100 percent responsible for my hustle, it only poured gasoline on the fire. My desire to do whatever it took found me inside my new entrepreneurial adventures because it was a pattern attached to a faulty belief I had adopted as truth.

Running myself ragged stemmed from the belief I was not worthy enough to prioritize. Because I didn't feel worthy, I needed other people to validate my existence. To obtain their praise, I was constantly chasing the wants, wishes and desires others had for me. As I chased the temporary affirmation others could give me, I was exhausting myself to meet the expectations of everyone around me.

It is not possible to meet the expectations of everyone because they are a constantly moving target. Each person's expectations for me were different and often conflicted with one another. For example, one of my former bosses wanted me to be a mini version of her, while her manager encouraged me to show up authentically. My husband wanted to have a third child, while my good friend thought two was just the right number. Visitors to our inn had various opinions about ways to make the experience even better. Some guests thought I should include dinner as an offering, while other travelers wanted scaled-back amenities more in line with a vacation rental.

Other people's expectations were impossible to meet simultaneously because they were all vastly different. The one-sided, whatever-it-takes hustle clouds over the one voice to whom you need to listen: yours.

After returning home from my soul-searching walk that Monday morning, I sat outside on our deck and turned off my phone. Instead of knocking out all the "urgent" items on my to-do list, I decided to prioritize listening to myself.

I enjoyed a hot cup of coffee, pulled my favorite orange quilt over my shoulders and watched the birds fly from tree to tree. I breathed in and out deeply, transporting myself into the present moment and repeating in my head, "Just this. Just this. Just this." My racing thoughts stopped as I slipped into the present moment of the actual life I was living. I decided to set aside the opinions and expectations of others and instead begin to identify my own opinions and the expectations I had for myself.

Through tears of awareness, I asked myself some important, long overdue questions, and listened to the answers from my own voice:

- What are the things that keep me healthy?
  *Walking, alone time, quiet, a clean bedroom, deep conversations, hot showers, regular meals and talking about my feelings*
- What are the real priorities in my life?
  *Family, adventure, bringing out the best in others, mental wellness and my gal tribe*
- What are the immediate ways I can get more of what I need?
  *Be willing to give up some control and hire staff for the Historic Browning*

I made a promise to myself: I would stop being a whatever-it-takes torchbearer. I also made a crucial mental shift to begin the journey of believing in my own worthiness. It started as an internal conversation, during which I determined all by myself what truly mattered to me. I prioritized what I needed in my life. The thoughts, feelings and opinions of others were completely removed from these priorities.

Creating a list of priorities turned out to be relatively easy for me. I have shared my priorities with people many times at networking events and business meetings. I even have mentioned them to guests of the inn. While my priorities were true, I was not aligning my time with this all-important list. I decided my list of priorities could no longer be artificial talking points and lip service. Instead, I made the decision that eighty percent of my commitments should align with what I truly cared about.

After dedicating four hours to this intensive exercise, I recognized there was not enough of me to go around. I was not able to meet all the demands of my life without shorting people and myself. I decided the first thing I needed to do was hire staff for The Browning. The amount of time I was spending managing the day-to-day operations was not allowing me to prioritize anything else on my list or in my life.

For too long, I told myself the story that I couldn't afford to hire staff. I thought it was irresponsible to spend money on employees when we were barely breaking even. Hiring staff was an additional expense for my business, and it could be risky. It was apparent, however, that it was the immediate near-term solution to make myself a priority.

Instead of wavering on this business decision as I normally would, I acted quickly. I talked with Harlen that evening regarding my newfound revelation about my priorities. We discussed how I wanted to stop doing whatever it takes and about the importance of balancing my life according to my priority list, not my to-do list. We knew this "whatever it takes" mantra led to my crisis. I let him know I was terrified to hire staff because we couldn't afford it. We considered where we could make cuts in our personal lives to enable us to afford a staff. That night, I created job descriptions and put them on recruiting sites. The following week, I interviewed multiple candidates.

Any reservations I had about hiring staff dissipated after the first week of adding two new people to my team. They learned the ropes quickly, contributed new ideas and elevated the customer-service experience. My staff gave me much-needed time off from the seven-day-a-week grind that was draining me and leading me back in the direction of crisis. They freed up my time to work on strategic, revenue-generating business decisions. The time I was now able to spend on these business opportunities more than made up for my employees' salaries.

Most importantly, I had my weekends back with my family. Harlen and I started going on date nights again. I was present at all my son's soccer games. I had my alone time in the morning without having to get up at 5:00 a.m. I had the ability to prioritize cleaning my own home. These changes created balance.

Spoiler alert: I still don't wash my hair very often. It's not to conserve time; it's because I just don't want to.

## From Me to You

*My* whatever-it-takes mindset led me into crisis. It was a self-sacrificing mantra that played out in every new story I chose. It was a destructive "truth" disguising itself as hard work and lending itself to an inordinate amount of praise. From the outside looking in, I was the high achiever who did whatever it took to be helpful and successful. I was the role model for having it all together.

Unfortunately, underneath this diehard work ethic was another "truth" that contributed to my crisis: I was not worthy enough to prioritize. I believed my purpose in life was to slowly disappear and magnify others. This belief led to a perpetual one-sided hustle. I gave until I was depleted.

Certain truths in your life have kept you foundationally stuck inside patterns that do not serve you. I call these toxic truths. Often, they have been part of your operating system for so long it's hard to understand how they even got there. Remember, if you do not do the internal work to change yourself, you will keep repeating the habits, patterns and routines that landed you crisis. Consider this the sign that you need to explore your toxic truths. This is the sign from your friend Liesl that it's time to get curious about the toxic truths that contribute to behaviors that keep you stuck.

How do you recognize the toxic truths that you need to reframe?

## To help you identify your own toxic truths, I'm going to share some of my personal examples:

**Toxic Truth No. 1:** You must do whatever it takes to be successful. Work hard while others sleep. You can sleep when you're dead. Be the best at everything you pursue. Do whatever it takes to get there.

**Toxic Truth No. 2:** You cannot trust yourself. You must seek external guidance regarding how you should live your life. The core of you is evil and nothing about you is good.

**Toxic Truth No. 3:** It's important for you to be pretty and skinny. Your external appearance determines your value.

Recognizing toxic truths is tricky. However, identifying them is critical to moving forward. I believe there are characteristics all toxic truths share. This is not an all-inclusive list of each of their characteristics, but they are themes I regularly see.

**Characteristic—Toxic truths often are created for you, not by you.** While there are truths we have foundationally accepted, typically they were put into our heads by external forces.

Here are how my toxic truths fit these criteria:

**Toxic Truth No. 1:** Corporate America created this toxic truth. To be successful, my corporate job wanted me to self-sacrifice.

**Toxic Truth No. 2:** My religion created this toxic truth. My church believed there was nothing good about you. There could only be good inside of you when you surrendered to a higher power.

**Toxic Truth No. 3:** Several forces created this toxic truth: beauty magazines, products marketed to women, pageants, and on and on.

**Characteristic—Toxic truths are partially true.** Some components of toxic truths are generally true; otherwise, we wouldn't have accepted them. There is some truth wrapped up inside the lie. The truth hooks us into accepting the toxic belief.

Here are how my toxic truths fit these criteria:

**Toxic Truth No. 1:**

*The truth:* Hard work and doing your best will lead to success. Having a good work ethic is something we should value.

*The lie:* You should do whatever it takes to be successful. You must sacrifice to be successful.

**Toxic Truth No. 2:**

*The truth:* A wise person has many counselors and is willing to learn from others. There is great value in learning from others. A wise person has their own opinions, but also seeks the advice of others.

*The lie:* You cannot ever trust yourself or your own opinions.

**Toxic Truth No. 3:**

*The truth:* It is important to take care of ourselves. Our body is nourished through self-care routines, such as exercising and eating healthy foods.

*The lie:* You must look a certain way to be considered valuable or beautiful.

**Characteristic—Toxic truths typically deal in absolutes.** When you are upholding your toxic truth, the answer is generally extreme. There are no shades of gray in these truths or times when the truth is applied differently depending on the circumstance.

Here are how my toxic truths fit these criteria:

**Toxic Truth No. 1:**

*Absolute:* Do whatever it takes no matter the cost. All successful people work themselves to death.

**Toxic Truth No. 2:**

*Absolute:* You must never trust yourself. All wisdom exists outside of you. There is nothing good about you.

**Toxic Truth No. 3:**

*Absolute:* Your only value is your beauty.

**Characteristic—Toxic Truths start as something small and grow into something much larger.** Toxic truths are cancerous and continue to grow with time. Acceptance of these toxic truths creates a snowball effect; eventually, the truth controls you.

Here are how my toxic truths fit these criteria:

**Toxic Truth No. 1:**

*Snowball Example:* You have an important project at work that likely will lead to a promotion. For this project, you kill yourself working sixty hours a week to get it across the line. You tell yourself, "I'm only going to work this hard on this project because it's crucial." However, when the next project is assigned, your boss praises the output of the last project. Because of her praise, you decide to put in sixty hours a week again for several months. You tell yourself, "Not every project will be this intense. I'll eventually gain seniority and won't have to work like this." After each project and subsequent promotion, you repeat the same lines. You become a vice president at the company and still have no personal life.

**Toxic Truth No. 2:**

*Snowball Example:* You are told at church there is nothing good about you. You are a wretched sinner who needs saved. You are told that taking credit for any of your good actions is not humble. Therefore, you begin to mirror the language of the Christians around you. Anytime you receive a compliment about your hard work, you repeat the acceptable lines, "I can't take credit for this. It's all the higher power working inside me." You start to believe you cannot trust yourself to make any decisions on your own. You must pray and ask people at your church for advice on every major decision you make. Eventually, you are scared to trust yourself in even the smallest decisions, like what restaurant you should patronize. You look to God, your pastor's interpretation of the Bible, and your church to make decisions for you.

Detecting the toxic truths in your life is critical to navigating away from crisis. These deeply embedded half-truths, which you have accepted as absolute truths, are not serving you. Your toxic truths will be different than mine; however, I hope these shared characteristics are helpful to you in uncovering the toxic truths that are keeping you stuck.

# Chapter 11

## Unimportant Voices

It had been more than a year since we opened the doors to the Historic Browning Inn. I am sitting in a pretentious and overly crowded lunch spot near my former workplace. A few weeks prior, I sent a message to two executives with whom I had worked asking them to meet for lunch. Mike and Julie are long-time mentors and friends.

On this day, I have asked them to come prepared to discuss the future of my business. It's a heavy topic for a one-and-a-half-hour lunch date, but I need their feedback. Throughout the past year, I've felt exceptionally lonely as a new entrepreneur. I'm used to collaborating inside an office and filtering ideas through people who are smarter than I am.

Without this, I have felt downright lost in my business and unsure which direction to head in the future. While Harlen has been with me every step of the way, he is still working full time to support our family. There is only so much support he can provide and still continue to maintain all his work responsibilities. The loneliness accompanying my new entrepreneurial station in life is paralyzing, and I need familiar mentorship to help me get unstuck.

For this lunch, I had put on a muted gray business-professional dress, black tights and black designer heels. I've returned to my former corporate costume and it is stifling. It's the middle of winter and I forgot how much I hate the feeling of itchy tights against my legs and wearing dreadfully uncomfortable heels, even if only for a couple of hours. I am revisiting a former life where I no longer belong.

In my past life, I was a high performer at a multi-billion-dollar company with executive potential, and now I make beds for a living. For a moment, I feel inadequate among the sea of professionals ordering expensive bottles of wine for lunch. While waiting in a corner booth for my former mentors, I ask the waitress for a plate of lemons for my water, then silently wonder if I have chosen the wrong life for my new chapter.

When my mentors arrive, I get up from the booth, give casual side hugs and thank them for taking the time to join me amid their busy schedules. Prior to this lunch meeting, I had emailed a mountain of business financials and asked if they could review these documents.

I've always been the dreamer, the visionary and the experience-maker. I am the jump-in-without- looking risktaker. Exploring the impossible is energizing and requires a certain lack of practicality. My financial acumen has always been a weakness, and I'm hoping Julie and Mike can bring their expertise to the table.

As we are ordering salads and catching up, I can't help but notice I'm the only one uncomfortable at the table. We had been together before in many, many meeting rooms and I was always at ease, but this meeting is different. There are a flurry of thoughts racing through my head. They don't know this version of me; they fell in love with the last iteration of me. I have evolved so much I might not be recognizable to them. What if they think the person I have become is lackluster in comparison?

Maybe I had chosen to wear an I-mean-business dress, itchy black tights and insufferable designer heels because this is what the person they had known would wear.

To maintain the comfort in our former relationship, I make the incorrect assumption I must impress them. I feel like a child who has left the nest and is returning home to justify her latest feats. I'm awkward, my palms are sweaty and I'm wondering why I was so bold to invite them. They have bigger things to worry about than my small dreams. Nonetheless, they are sitting in front of me, which is an action that communicates, "We still care." I have absolutely nothing to offer them, yet they are still here.

Julie, sensing my nervousness, takes control of the conversation. "What do you want to talk about today, Liesl?"

I pull out printed copies of the Historic Browning's financials from the first year and place them next to their salads. Our corporate meetings together always required a stack of printed handouts with folders and pens. I want to appear organized and structured to show I'm not wasting their time. I begin rambling on about where the business stands financially after year one, trying to avoid the fact we lost money.

Mike stops me. "Let's try this again. We're both impressed by what you've done after leaving. I reviewed your financials, and you lost money in year one. That's normal for a new business. What do you really need help with?"

Mike's simple question invites me to authentically show up to the table with them. I look at my former mentors and really see them for the first time. Mike is wearing jeans and a collared shirt. Julie is in a casual turtleneck. Instead of the pretentious bottles of wine being poured around us, Julie orders an Arnold Palmer, her usual.

I remember the first time I met Julie and she offered me peanuts and water out of her small, outdated early-1990s office. One time when we were running late to the corporate jet, she bought Mike his favorite chicken wings from a local grocery store to make amends. When Mike and I were preparing his presentation for the executive forum, he spent hours thinking about how to make it meaningful for his audience. This is how they always show up: approachable, non-pretentious and willing to help.

Suddenly, my business professional attire and stack of financials seem silly.

All the walls come down and I am honest with them about my business struggles. I tell them I'm totally lost, have no idea what I'm doing and I'm lonely. I know these financials should mean something and give me direction, but I don't know where to focus. I have all these ideas swirling in my head and no clue what to prioritize. I tell them I'm stuck and have even thought about selling the business because I feel unfit to manage it.

After revealing my truth, Mike says, "What do you believe should be your focus for the Historic Browning in 2018?"

An exceptionally long tangent follows, with me regurgitating all the advice I've been given recently. I tell them about a fellow business owner who has big ideas for totally reimagining the space at the Historic Browning. There's also a potential guest who sent a Facebook message to me and believes if I invested in a pool and hot tub more people would stay at my inn. A few banker friends think I should take out a loan to convert the attached garage into a carriage house. My neighbor thinks there will never be a market for an inn in downtown Lee's Summit and that I should sell the property.

I pause to catch my breath. Apparently, breathing is an important thing to do when you're talking your face off.

"That's a lot of advice for someone who is lonely," Mike says. "No wonder you're lacking direction. Maybe the real problem is that you have too much advice from the wrong people. You have no idea what direction to head because you haven't prioritized whose advice matters."

Mike has always stunned me with his sage advice. He's one of the quietest people in the room until he believes it's time to speak up. When he does, he typically offers the most thought-provoking contribution. The reason I appreciate him so much is because the stark contrast between us provides a depth of perspective. Mike sits with his thoughts internally, like slowly swirling his wine in the glass until the richness of flavor peeks.

I blurt out my unpolished thoughts externally, hoping someone can help me sort through the meaning. "How do you prioritize whose opinion matters?"

Mike finishes his thought, "When you look at the people who've dispensed an inordinate amount of advice, do you want to be like any of them? Do you even like them? Do you want your life to be like theirs?"

I thought we would be talking about profit and loss statements, but this conversation has veered into an entirely new direction. I begin to noodle over these profound questions.

Mike walks me through each person on the list and asks me what I think of them.

- **Fellow Business Owner:** While I genuinely like him as a person, he has several businesses he manages and owns. He's a serial entrepreneur and is focused heavily on monetizing everything he touches. While I'm sure his advice is solid if my predominate goal is making money, I don't want my business life to look like his. It doesn't mean he's a bad human; I just don't aspire to be him.
- **Potential guest:** I know nothing about this person. She has never stayed at the Historic Browning and I've never met her. I don't have enough information to determine if her opinion matters to my business.
- **Bank advisors:** The acquaintances I know who work in baking are sharp individuals who are always willing to offer advice. Their lives, however, are spent working inside banking institutions that profits if I take out another loan. While I'm certain they have my best interest at heart, it's hard for them to look at my situation objectively.
- **Neighbor down the street:** I quickly eliminate the advice of my neighbor who works sixty hours a week and lives for his weekends. I don't want my life to look like his at all.

"I haven't been seeking advice from the people whose opinions matter to me," I blurt out. "That's why I'm so lost. Everyone's opinion matters; therefore, no one's opinion matters. I haven't surrounded myself with people I respect and want to be like."

Julie smiles as I unravel these truths in front of them.

Sitting in front of me are two humble, kind, successful and brilliant humans. They've owned businesses and invested in businesses. They each have meaningful relationships with their families. Most of all, they have my best interests at heart.

The rest of our lunch was spent brainstorming ideas for The Browning. We discussed every possible scenario that existed inside different possibilities: selling the business, growing the business or changing it into something else. We remained open to all possibilities.

From that day forward, I gave each new piece of advice from people the attention it actually deserved. If the advice came from trusted sources who had my best interests at heart, I listened. If the advice came from people I did not want to be like or I did not really know, I put those opinions in my unimportant voices file.

## From Me to You

There is no shortage of opinions in this world. Scroll through social media on any given day and dive in. What you'll find are the thoughts, feelings and beliefs of hundreds of people, many of whom you haven't even talked to since high school. You know little to nothing about most of these people. Yet, we often give these people an inordinate amount of our attention.

It is easy to get lost in the opinions of others. Every single one of us has let someone else's viewpoint take us in a direction we didn't want to go. When we consistently prioritize the thoughts, feelings and opinions of others above our own, we eventually begin living stories we don't recognize. We become a collection of what everyone else wants and not what we want. While feedback from others is generally well intentioned, it doesn't mean it is right for you.

For many of us, abandoning the stories that resonate deep within our soul because of what someone else believes is right for us occurs one decision at a time. A single decision to abandon one of your stories can seem minor; after all, it's only the act of abandoning one thing in your life that felt true. However, a collection of these decisions sits between you and the life you genuinely want. After living the new stories that others suggested for us, many of us find ourselves in crisis. We look at our lives and recognize we made every decision that led to this point, but it still doesn't feel like our life.

Maybe you've found yourself in a similar situation and have asked yourself the deepest of soul-searching questions: Wasn't my life supposed to be more than this?

You will never escape the opinions of others. You can only control how much weight you give them. I believe one of the biggest steps we can take to living our lives authentically is to stop listening to the opinions of people who do not truly matter to us.

While deciding whose opinions mattered to me began as a business exercise, it served as an important personal lesson as well. Harlen and I became so fascinated with this topic we spent several of our couple's walks focused on it.

We came up with a list of categories that helped us decide the opinions that mattered to us and the ones that did not. Harlen put on his nerdy data science thinking cap and even suggested we assign weight to the advice each person gives us. I humored him.

## Harlen and I defined four categories that help us determine the weight of someone's advice and opinions:

- **Category 1: People we don't ever want to be like.** This is by far the easiest category to identify. There are people in our lives who we don't want to be like at all. They are completely uninspiring to us and we wouldn't trade lives with them for any amount of money.

  One example is the neighbor who thought we should sell the inn. In his current life state and circumstances, his feedback about how I should live my life or run my business holds no weight. His advice, therefore, was assigned zero points in my personal "Advice I Do Not Care About" bucket. How do you identify individuals who fit in this category? These are the people you look at and say, "Their life is way far off from the one I want to live. I would never take their advice."

  The advice of these people should become white noise to you. Don't waste any of your time or headspace on the opinions freely dispensed from people in this category. When their advice is provided, simply smile, nod and say "Thanks." Then, as quickly as it hit your ears, let it exit your thoughts. Important note: At any given point in time, we ourselves fit into this category for others. When my life was in total ruin and crisis, I imagine no one wanted to take advice from me.

- **Category 2: People I admire, but don't want to be like in the area they are providing advice:** This is by far the hardest category to identify. Often, these are the individuals from whom we take advice that ends up being wrong for us. For me, this was the successful downtown business owner who prioritized the bottom line. Overall, he is a decent human being and his intent was to genuinely help me. Furthermore, he has had several successful businesses and is well known in our community. However, once I dug deeper and truly reflected, I recognized that I do not aspire to run my business like he does.

I didn't pursue the entrepreneurial life to become exceptionally wealthy and monetize everything I touch. My core motivation for going out on my own was to provide healing for my family, as well as comfort and enjoyment for the people who visit our inn. Many times, I prioritize the experience at the Historic Browning over profit because my core motivations are different than this other downtown business owner. While I don't want to lose money, I would be content to break even at The Browning. While the business owner's advice is not wrong, it is wrong for me. Our core motivations for owning our businesses are different. This business owner's advice received an average weight. While I recognize there are probably nuggets of wisdom that I can glean from him, I weigh his words cautiously. I weigh everything he says against my own core value system to see if it fits.

How do you identify individuals who fit in this category? You must dig deep to answer these questions: What core motivations does this person have in the area for which they are providing advice to me? What are my core motivations in the area for which they are providing advice? What do I want my life to look like in this area? What does their life look like in this area?

After you've thought through these questions and answered them, it should help clarify the weight you assign this advice. Perhaps there are areas in which you can still learn from these individuals if you sift through the parts that are authentic to you. Consider the weight of this advice carefully.

- **Category 3: People who have ulterior motives in the area for which they are providing advice:** There will always be people who provide advice and have ulterior motives. Sometimes the person knows they have ulterior motives; other times they do not. For instance, my banker friends are genuinely upstanding people who want to help me. They are always willing to brainstorm business ideas and their advice is well-meaning. However, they cannot help but view my problem through the lens from which is they are looking: They are bankers first and my friends and acquaintances second.

When I was struggling to make loan payments in my first year, their advice was to finish our garage into a carriage house and take out another loan to make it happen. While I believe the intention was to help me grow my business, their view was slightly skewed in relationship to my goals. I wanted to increase revenue at the inn without needing to make major modifications or take out another loan. Furthermore, my problem wasn't the need for additional rooms, it was the need to fill the rooms I already had. I assigned my banker friends' advice zero points.

People with ulterior motives aren't necessarily providing advice with malicious intent. I like to believe they rarely do. But it's important to analyze the lens through which someone is seeing your problem and to ask important questions, such as: What does this person have to gain if I choose to act on their specific advice? Through what lens is this advice-giver seeing my problem?

After you have answered these questions, assign the necessary weight you would give their advice. In my situation, I discarded the well-meaning advice of my banker confidants based on the knowledge that they were narrowly viewing my problem through their lens, not mine. If I had taken out another loan on top of the one that I already was having a hard time paying, my business certainly would have collapsed after year two. Instead, I prioritized targeted-marketing efforts to increase my book of business for bridal parties, which was my highest revenue-generating area. I did spend some money to do this, but it wasn't a $40k renovation.

- **Category 4: People for whom I don't have enough information about them:** This category is simple to identify. A lot of advice you receive comes from people you know little to nothing about. One example of this is the potential guest who sent a message to me recommending I add a pool and a hot tub to my inn's amenities. I didn't know this person at all and she had never stayed at the inn. This feedback received a weight of zero. Guests of the inn who I know personally or who have experience in my industry also have offered advice, and I weigh each of their opinions based on the same questions I use for people in the other categories.

If you regularly take advice from people who you don't really know, it will exhaust you. Being captive to the thoughts, feelings and opinions of people with whom you rarely interact is a huge waste of time. Save your headspace. This also goes for the people on social media who you have not seen since high school.

- **Category 5: People I want to be like in the area for which they are providing advice:** These individuals are the sweet spot. Listening to their feedback will support you in living your life authentically. For me, these individuals were my former mentors Mike and Julie. They had a great deal of experience in the area for which they were offering their advice to me. They also had my best interests at heart and were removed enough from the situation as to have zero ulterior motives.

The best partners to have when exploring feedback are individuals who know your personal goals. They know you well enough to understand what you value, and they can coach you to arrive at the end result that is best for you. Mike and Julie worked through a variety of different scenarios with me and remained open to each one possibly being right for me. My mentors' advice received a pretty "10" from me.

Maintaining relationships with a small group of people who can provide insight into various topics is critical. Ultimately, I believe the deep workings of our inner voice guide us in the right direction to discover the counsel of advisors who can help us see things from all angles and who you want to emulate. These are the best people to pull in when we are feeling absolutely lost and have no idea which direction to head.

Initially, the practice of categorizing the advice you receive can be difficult. As someone who used to listen to the thoughts, feelings and opinions of almost everyone, it took me more practice than it might take you. In the beginning, it was easiest for me to identify the people I did not want to be like, as well as the individuals for whom I did have enough information to know if their advice was valuable or not. If you are attempting to mute unimportant voices and their advice, I recommend starting with those two categories.

When you begin to recognize the people whose voices and advice you no longer give much weight, the opinions of those who do matter to you will become more apparent. Over time, this won't be much of an exercise at all. With practice, you'll be able to easily identify the opinions you care about and the ones you do not. The result: You'll begin living your life on your own terms.

If you're ready to rearrange your life, join me in Part III: Rearranged.

# Part III:
## Rearranged

*Sometimes you have put your world into such a brilliant new order, you see life in spring colors: whimsical teals, airy yellows and lively greens. You are enamored with all the growth around you and all the growth you created from doing the hard work. You have rearranged your life to reflect the truest version of who you are in this moment. In this phase, life feels authentic, free and beautiful.*

## Chapter 12
# *Funeral Goals*

---❤---

*If the measure of a good life is constancy of purpose and com-mitment, unconditional love of family, lifelong friendships and meaningful action, then Pop lived well. Pop's life was dedicated to his family, his faith and our country.*

Sitting in a pew at St. Patrick's Catholic Church in Galveston, Texas, in December 2017, I observed that nearly every pew inside the exquisite and expansive cathedral was filled. My uncle Terry was reading one of the most heartfelt eulogies I have ever heard.

Three days prior, I was furiously prepping for a bridal party at the Historic Browning Inn. Amid the chaos of getting every-thing ready, my mom called. My grandfather, whom we called Pawpaw, had passed away. This phone call came as no surprise to me, but it was still a difficult moment. My Pawpaw was nine-ty-two years old.

The year prior, his wife, Bunnie, our Mimi, had passed away and he was never the same after she was gone. While it was his time to leave this earth, the news of his permanent absence from our lives was surreal.

As the news sunk in, I was both sad and relieved. During the past year, my Pawpaw's physical and mental health had declined. The bright, spirited and kind man I fell in love with had an increasingly vacant look behind his eyes. He seemed angry. When my Mimi departed the world, so did Pawpaw's recognizable spark. Throughout their long marriage, they had never spent a Christmas apart. He died on December 23, just in time to meet his bride in heaven for Christmas.

As I left The Browning that day, I was feeling a combination of emotions. I had little time to work through them because of the urgency to make arrangements to attend the funeral in Galveston. My staff would have to manage The Browning in my absence, and there was a significant amount of delegation and trust to pull it all off. Up until this point, I was the primary client-facing employee at the inn, especially for bridal parties.

When I returned home from the inn, Harlen and I began making plans for my travel, discussed schedules, and called all the staff to ask for additional coverage during the weekend. The last call I made was to the bride getting married at The Browning to transition her experience to my staff. She was gracious, understanding and kind as I explained the situation.

Everyone came through for me with overwhelming support so I could be in the place where I was most needed. It was the first time I had left my "baby," the Historic Browning, in the care of others, and I felt incredibly vulnerable. While I was creating detailed work instructions that evening, Harlen assured me he would take good care of both our family and the business in my absence.

The following day, my dad, mom, sister and I headed to the airport to fly to Galveston. While sitting in the airport terminal, I was reminded of my childhood. I couldn't remember the last time the four of us had traveled together, but our time together felt both familiar and a somewhat distant part of our past.

"During high school, he met Bunnie Louise Hawkins on a blind date and *that* was *that*. He told his mother the next morning that he met the girl he was going to marry. He was wise for his age, as they were together for the rest of their lives," said Uncle Terry as he continued the eulogy.

As my uncle spoke, I was furiously pulling Kleenex out of my small purse that was wedged in between myself and my sister, Marta. I have always been a deeply feeling person who expresses her emotions freely, but I was trying not to sob. I didn't want my cries to overpower the beautiful eulogy being delivered. My sister, who rarely cries in public, was about to let it all out.

I could see her out of the corner of my eye. She is a private person, so I tried not to look at her. She needed this moment to herself to internally process everything she was feeling. As much as I wanted to put my arm around her and cry together, I knew this wasn't her way.

My dad and mom were in the pew in front of us. There were multiple rows of our family. My Pawpaw and Mimi had eight children and several grandchildren. Looking down the rows of family members and the packed church, I was hard-pressed to find a dry eye in the house.

"He was a walking encyclopedia of Galveston families, and if you met him, before long you were talking about your grandfather's or grandmother's or uncle's family and where they worked and where they lived and what sport they played and who they married, which took you down a whole other road. He took an interest in people and their histories. He was sincere."

As my uncle spoke, I was transported back to one of my favorite memories of my grandfather. When we were growing up, my sister and I were the only grandchildren who didn't live nearby. I often longed to be a part of the stories and many adventures with Pawpaw that my cousins would tell me about. When he came to visit us, he would sneak my sister and me fifty-dollar bills.

This tradition carried into adulthood. I distinctly remember one of his last visits to Manhattan, Kansas, where my parents lived. I was in my late twenties, with one small child and pregnant with my second. Pawpaw snuck me back into my parent's kitchen, pulled me in for a big hug, and slyly slipped fifty dollars into my hand. He always made me smile. I never doubted how much I mattered to him.

When my uncle closed out his poignantly written eulogy, I breathed in the collective energy of the people around me. Our grandfather's life was a legacy. I believe when he reached paradise, God patted him on the back and said, "Well done, my good and faithful servant."

After the memorial service, we all attended the wake. My family always knows how to host an exceptional party. They had rented space at a local seafood establishment and no detail was overlooked. There was an open bar, a buffet line of incredible food and the company of all the people who mattered most in Pawpaw's life.

I was heading to the bar, but having a difficult time making it there. On the hunt for a glass of Merlot, various friends and family who wanted to share memories were stopping me along the way. I listened to each story, intently collecting the meaningful moments that marked my Pawpaw's life.

After getting my wine and finally sitting down to eat, a group of my cousins began recanting a collection of moments our Pawpaw had given to us—from Texas A&M Aggie football games and fishing trips to fifty-dollar bills and large Christmas morning gatherings at my grandparents' home. Each one of us had been given a series of stories we could hold onto.

After the wake, I went to my cousin Jennifer's house where I was staying. I took a hot shower, got ready for bed and called my family back in Missouri to say goodnight. I shared with them some of the highlights of the day and my favorite Pawpaw memory. Before heading downstairs to spend time with my cousin and her husband, I sat on the bed for a few moments and reflected on the powerful eulogy my uncle had delivered. I revisited the memories, the stories and the collection of moments shared among the people who knew my Pawpaw best.

The awe-inspiring tribute had conjured up deep meaning for me. I reflected on what makes our lives meaningful: stories, memories, advice, love, time, attention. A funeral is a celebration of life, a celebration of their stories.

I could not stop thinking about one particular line from the eulogy that was a quote from my Pawpaw.

"He would often say, 'Don't tell me what your priorities in life are, just tell me where you spend your time . . . those are your priorities, whether you like it or not.'"

My Pawpaw's priorities were never lip service. He didn't merely rattle off about how much he loved his wife and family, then barely spend time with them. When he owned a successful small business, work did not consume his every waking moment. When he was at work, he focused on work. When he was with his family, he focused on his family. He didn't need to loudly proclaim all his priorities; his actions revealed what truly mattered to him.

From serving as the volunteer coach for football and baseball teams to rarely missing his children's and grandchildren's activities, he aligned his time to his life priorities. If there was ever a question about what he truly valued, all you had to do was step into his funeral.

Sitting in the pews that day were a collection of all the people to whom he gave his attention. Every person inside Saint Patrick's that day knew how much they mattered to my grandfather. On that December day, my Pawpaw had gathered his big family together one last time, allowing us to say goodbye. His actions and his life reminded me of the truest, most beautiful thing we can give to one another: our undivided attention.

## From Me to You

You might not believe your funeral matters much. After all, you won't even be there to witness it. It's possible you're wondering why I even brought up such an overused sentiment. I wouldn't be the first self-development author to ask you to judiciously consider your funeral (we're a little weird like that).

Whenever I am pursuing long-term planning of any kind, I take the advice of one of the smartest executives at my former corporate job. He would always say, "Visualize a vivid description of how a future state in time will look, then work backward."

When I am trying to figure out where I should be focusing my attention, I envision my funeral. I don't envision it forty years in the future, I imagine it's happening in five years. Even my wisest of counselors at work never advised planning forty years out. Instead, we always planned five years at time.

Are your current priorities and actions aligning to your five-year funeral goals?

Many of us have priorities we communicate outwardly at social events, during work meetings, on social media and to single-serving friends we meet on airplanes. We rattle off the words we're expected to say: "I'm married to my amazing husband, Harlen. We have two kids, Mady and Ethan, and they are my everything."

I recited these words even in the middle of my affair. Obviously, my actions were in significant misalignment with my so-called priorities. It's possible you're thinking, "Lady, how could you be having an affair and still say those words?"

I believe it's because I desperately wanted these overtures to be true, but underneath, when I drilled down deeply, I recognized an aching. This aching is a subtle reminder we are lacking a commitment to the things that really matter.

Many of us justify our late nights at the office and missed moments of being fully present under the guise that "we're doing it for all for our families" or another important priority. For me, two things motivated me to want to get ahead in my job: my need for achievement and the false belief that with more money, I could give my children the life they deserved. What I personally failed to realize until later was that my family wanted the gift of my attention more than any elaborate trip, expensive pair of shoes or the highest-end trampoline in the neighborhood.

Balancing multiple priorities isn't easy, but it is part of our lives. There are points in our life when one thing needs to take priority over another. Sometimes, the high-visibility project at work temporarily takes a front seat to family dinner. Other times, a good friend has a major life event that requires a significant amount of support. There are moments when a partner loses a loved one and all the focus and energy moves there. These temporary adjustments are necessary. However, when our life becomes hyper-focused on one priority for too long, imbalance is the result.

Like most things in life, a continued commitment to one priority doesn't happen all at once; it occurs one small decision after another small decision after another. Eventually, these decisions pile up, then one day you're standing inside a sea of cubicles for the 100th late night in a row, when the executive you loathe and who you never want to be like walks down your aisle, gives you a high five and says, "Look at us doing whatever it takes to get ahead. We'll work while they sleep. Keep hustling!" (Clearly not a personal example, wink wink.)

These micro-decisions become the story of your life. You missed just one more soccer game, one more wedding, one more recital, one more dinner and one more celebration. Now you find yourself living a life you don't want. The power of your attention can become laser focused on things that are not a priority in your life. This often leaves you perplexed because you are wholeheartedly certain of what truly matters in your life; you sputter it off ad-nauseum anytime someone asks.

Here is a reminder for you: Attention is one of the most powerful things you can give to your people, your priorities and your life focus.

The power of your attention is so magnificent, people fight for it all the time. Newspapers, radio, TV, websites, social media and apps are all trying to get your attention. It is so valuable because companies profit off it regularly. There is never really a free game, free app or free download. Most complimentary items you consume are a trade. In addition to collecting data, the commodity these companies are constantly seeking is your focus, which is what you give them as the tradeoff.

Here is one of the most empowering truths: The magic of your focus is 100 percent in your control. Every morning, you have a fresh supply to give, and you can allot it however you choose. Sure, you inevitably need to meet certain priorities, like going to work, but there is still enough focus left to create meaningful eulogy-worthy moments. Here's an even more marvelous truth: Your attention doesn't cost you anything.

At one grand and final party to celebrate my Pawpaw's life, he was not finished speaking. He reminded me of the real power of attention. An entire church full of admiring people to whom he had intentionally given his energy were the recipients of his focused attention. Every person in that room was given the rarest commodity any person can supply to another human: a moment of their focus. That attention turns into stories that transition into memories that end in eulogy-worthy moments.

To what are you giving your attention? Does it align with your life priorities?

## Here are a few things that help me prioritize my focus:

- **Create a priority list**. You might inherently know your priorities, but creating a thoughtful list supports clarity. Plus, it gives you time to explore priorities deeper than the surface. Spend time going beyond the usual answers you share in single-dose interactions at social gatherings or on social media. If you only stick with the list that comes mechanically when you're speaking to others, you'll miss out. Once you create your initial priority list, I challenge you to go even deeper. Think outside of what you originally wrote down. The easiest way to do this is sitting with the exercise. Anytime you think you're done, spend five minutes more thinking about it again. Do this at least three times and you'll uncover some answers you didn't expect.

- **Do an attention inventory**. When you are done creating your priority list, estimate the weekly amount of time you spend in each priority area. Again, it is one thing to say you prioritize something, but it is entirely another to in fact align your time and attention accordingly. Make sure you honestly assess where you are at with your time and attention. No one is going to see or judge this inventory except you. Once you are finished, determine the areas where you need to dedicate more time.

- **Create funeral goals**: Imagine your funeral is five years away. Create a vivid description of this future state in a way that is meaningful to you (written word, picture, song, etc.). Identify the people who will be there and what you want them to say about you. Revisit the collateral you created for this exercise at least once a year to make edits when necessary.

## Chapter 13
# Trampoline Freedom

---

I t was a hot, sticky summer evening in June 2018. It had been two years since we first began dreaming up our plans to open the Historic Browning Inn, but it felt as though I had lived more life in this short timespan than in the past five years.

The deep emotional work that was part of the journey had been grueling, but undoubtedly meaningful. During this time, our family had experienced heartache, loss, new beginnings, healing, renewal and transformation. Some parts of us were the same, many were completely rearranged.

That June day was particularly long at The Browning. A powerful storm had caused a massive power outage throughout the downtown area, rendering the inn with no power. To add to the frustration, the community's annual three-day Downtown Days Festival also was without power. The event draws thousands of people to our downtown and it brings several guests to our inn every year. Without the festival operating, all our booked guests cancelled their stays. Apparently, people value air conditioning in their guest rooms. Who knew?

As a new business relying heavily on the high revenue-generating summer months, it was emotionally frustrating to be powerless against the weather and worrisome to lose the revenue. On a positive note, however, this minor catastrophe had given me an extremely rare weekend off.

As I began contemplating what to do with an entire forty-eight hours to spend with my family, Harlen called. He wanted to grill hamburgers for the family and eat outside on the patio. It sounded like the perfect start to the weekend. What had I done to deserve a weekend off and someone else managing dinner?

In preparation for our al fresco dinner, I wiped down the patio furniture and furiously sweep around it. Heading back into the house, I checked in with the kids, then poured myself a large glass of pinot grigio, grabbed my earbuds and returned to the patio to sip wine and listen to music. I got comfortable in one of our oversized rattan chairs and draped my legs over the arm. Taking in a deep breath, I paused for a moment and thought to myself, "I'm happy. Right now, in this moment, I'm happy."

It was hard to believe that only two years prior, I was in the thick of crisis. The woman who drove away from her corporate life now seems like a foreigner to me, nearly inaccessible in certain ways. It feels as though there are thousands of years between that woman and me, and one of us now possesses more wisdom than she can fathom. I am certain the woman who was barely managing to get through life could have ever imagined this beautiful and still summer moment.

## Today

While the woman I was and the woman I am today are far removed from one another, I can still channel the raw emotions that accompanied her when she had hit the bottom. When crisis entered my life, it was a heartache that was released in between screaming cries and gasping breaths. On that last day at my corporate job, when I packed up what felt like the entirety of my life into one measly cardboard box, I could not see beyond those current circumstances. I believed everyone except me knew the secret to life. Somehow, most of the world population had received carefully crafted "Live Your Best Life" instructions delivered to their door. Mine never arrived.

The woman who lived inside that former story believed brokenness meant it was the end of her life. In contrast, the woman draped over the rattan armchair knew brokenness was exactly what she had needed. Hindsight is by far the greatest teacher. If that former woman could have accessed this future happy moment on her patio, she would have seen there was life after brokenness. But first she needed to be broken, changed, and rearranged to arrive at this moment.

Brokenness awakened me to a fundamental truth my soul had always known: Every phase of this life is richly beautiful, worthy and meant for us to experience. When we run from the fullness of being completely human, we are living in denial. All phases of life and the emotions we experience are teachers. Without the contrast of the full spectrum of these experiences, our lives would lack true depth.

**Broken:** Sometimes the colors of our lives are like winter—muted grays, dull whites and shadowy blacks. We are hard-pressed to understand our current circumstances and wonder if the darkness will ever end. It's normal in this phase to ponder when we will ever feel alive again. Oftentimes, survival is all we can manage, and it would be wise to accept that as a true accomplishment. The death of old patterns, routines and things that no longer serve us prepares us for richer and more beautiful things to come. It prepares us for what will come next: change.

**Changed:** Other times, life is lived through the colors of fall—rich maroons, bright oranges and vibrant yellows. As fall beckons change, it signals it is time to release the things in our life that no longer add to its beauty. In this phase, we clear out old patterns, beliefs and ways of doing things that no longer serve us. This magical season prepares us to make space to rearrange our lives in a more authentic way. This phase allows us to reevaluate what we want, get rid of the things we do not, and make space to rearrange.

**Rearranged:** Then there are the times when you have put your life into such a brilliant new order, you see the world in spring colors—whimsical teals, airy yellows and lively greens. You are enamored with all the growth around you and all the growth you created from doing the hard work.

You have rearranged your life to reflect the truest version of who you are in this moment in time. In this phase, life feels authentic, free and beautiful.

Each phase is an equal teacher and a contributor to the process of continually becoming truer, then becoming truer again and becoming truer again. Evolution after evolution.

On that summer evening, two years after surviving the most difficult part of my life, I was overwhelmed with feelings of gratitude that came squarely from the rearranged phase. My dramatic growth was the result of surviving the broken phase and embracing the changed phase. My marriage was on the right path. I was spending more time with my children. I cherished a small group of friends. I had a business I loved. And I finally felt happy again. I had rearranged everything in my life to reflect the most current iteration I needed.

Feeling so much gratitude inspired me to jump out of the rattan patio chair, flippantly chuck my bright orange flip-flops onto the grass and wiggle my bare feet in dry dirt. I scrolled for one of my favorite songs on my phone and cranked up the music as loud as it would go. I closed my eyes, threw my arms up into the air and started twirling around. The wild of the wind ran through each one of my fingers. I started to dance, or at least it was a form of movement that might not exactly be called dancing. I think my emotional, physical and mental body finally intersected in harmony and the result was unencumbered freedom. I felt unhinged and free.

Neighbors were all around me enjoying the evening from their back decks and patios. I paid them no mind. The intensity of being wrapped up in this rearranged moment moved me to next pull myself up onto my children's trampoline. This required an acrobatic feat, and I imagine I looked like a seal trying to maneuver through unfamiliar territory and pushing myself up on my hands in an ungraceful and slightly undignified way.

In this moment, the trampoline felt like the only thing that could align my physical self with the unfettered freedom my mental self was experiencing. I felt weightless in the air as I bounced up and down like a seven-year-old.

I heard the screaming laugher of my children running outside to meet me. They were undoubtedly amused to see their mother romping around the trampoline. The number of times they had asked me to jump with them in the past are too many to count. I hadn't been free enough then. The kids climbed up on the black rubbery surface with me and we began bouncing up and down together.

We listened to '90s music, played silly trampoline games, and they laughed like children do—and so did I. After about thirty minutes of this childhood frivolity, I wet my pants and my side hurt more than I care to mention. Perhaps my mental and physical body weren't as aligned as I thought.

When I got off the trampoline that night, my husband was grateful I was still in one piece—a huge accomplishment for his clumsy, trampoline-jumping, pushing forty-year-old wife. My trampoline antics resulted in zero trips to the emergency room, so the weekend was off to a good start. We ate dinner that night on the patio outside, shared stories about the day, discussed the importance of adults jumping on the trampoline every now and then, and simply enjoyed each other's company and being together.

One day, I hope you feel free enough to jump on a trampoline like no one is watching you. My prayer for you is that you embrace every phase of your life that led to each moment of your current transformation. I hope you can taste freedom in the air as you freefall into the juicy, beautiful life that is meant for you.

During your glorious trampoline moments, I also hope you never stop and wonder for even a single second what your neighbors are thinking about the spectacle.

## From Me to You

I hope this book helps you feel seen, understood, loved and whole. It has been one of the hardest, yet meaningful works of my life. The construction of each sentence has been a true labor of love. I believe it was meant for both you and for me. Creating this book has been a healing outlet for me, and I hope it is a source of healing for you as well.

I hope this book taught you the importance of small circles and the value of people who love you through difficult times. Don't ever lose sight of these people because they are the greatest loves of your life. Your crisis-proof friendships are worth investing your time and energy. Prioritize them above all others.

I hope you walked away recognizing there is true power in owning your story and coming to the table just as you are. This is the foundation for all intimacy—not only intimacy with others, but also with yourself. Everything that exists outside the sacredness of owning your truth is a one-sided hustle that will leave you burned out and lonely. Hold yourself accountable to show-ing up as your whole self every day.

You will be rejected by many, but these are not your people. When you have hurt someone you love, recognize the ability to be honest with yourself and with them about the hurt you have caused. This will be foundational for the healthy relationships we all need and deserve.

I hope this book gave you the tools you need to silence unimportant voices in your life. Once you stop obsessing about people who you do not even want to be like, you will experience a freedom you never knew. With so much more space in your head, you can focus on the things that matter to you. I encourage you to fill that extra headspace with the voices of people who do matter and the dreams that matter to you. In return, you will begin to live authentically. Seriously, it will be life changing.

Mostly, I hope this book gave you the courage to love your-self deeply and honor your true inner voice. My prayer is that it showed you how ludicrous it is to allow others to define the life you should live. Only you can determine the life you are meant to live. No matter how much a community, neighborhood, soci-ety, church, colleagues and social groups strive to define what is right for your life, you are the only person who really knows.

Do not be afraid to tap into your inner voice who knows how to keep you healthy. This will always be the key to finding the next story you were meant to live, and the one after that, and the one after that.

Here's to each evolution getting a tad more beautiful,
Liesl

# Let's Write Our Stories Together.

believe many of us are living stories that were created for us and not by us. Then, we wonder why we walk around feeling half alive. Crisis taught me: Life will begin the moment you agree to write your own story. I hope this book inspired you to begin.

Let's continue to write our stories together.

Here are a few ways I'd love to stay connected:

- **Resources and Tools:** There are a variety of resources and tools to support you in each phase of growth (Broken, Changed, and Rearranged). You can locate these free resources at: lieslhays.com/resources.

- **Be Social:** I'd love to continue the conversation on social media. You can connect with me on Instagram @liesl. hays or on Facebook at facebook.com/lieslhaysauthor

- **Share your stories:** I'd love to hear your personal stories and experiences of transformation. E-mail me at Lieslhays@lieslhays.com

# About the Author

L iesl Hays is a word artist, truth-teller, choice-maker, and inspirer.

For over a decade, Liesl has been facilitating training, mentoring others, and creating development experiences that require people to dig deep. She is an entrepreneur, inn owner, and human resources consultant.

Liesl runs on coffee, "to do lists," and the belief life begins after you agree to write your own story. She lives in Lee's Summit, Missouri with her husband, Harlen, her children, Mady and Ethan, and their dogs, Lily and Bear.

# A free ebook edition is available with the purchase of this book.

**To claim your free ebook edition:**

1. Visit MorganJamesBOGO.com
2. Sign your name CLEARLY in the space
3. Complete the form and submit a photo of the entire copyright page
4. You or your friend can download the ebook to your preferred device

Morgan James BOGO™

A **FREE** ebook edition is available for you or a friend with the purchase of this print book.

CLEARLY SIGN YOUR NAME ABOVE

**Instructions to claim your free ebook edition:**
1. Visit MorganJamesBOGO.com
2. Sign your name CLEARLY in the space above
3. Complete the form and submit a photo of this entire page
4. You or your friend can download the ebook to your preferred device

## Print & Digital Together Forever.

Snap a photo

Free ebook

Read anywhere

Printed in the USA
CPSIA information can be obtained
at www.ICGtesting.com
JSHW022334140824
68134JS00019B/1469